ALICE
WALKER

COMPREHENSIVE RESEARCH
AND STUDY GUIDE

BLOOM'S

MAJOR

NOVELISTS

EDITED AND WITH AN
INTRODUCTION BY HAROLD BLOOM

ALICE
WALKER

COMPREHENSIVE RESEARCH
AND STUDY GUIDE

BLOOM'S
MAJOR
NOVELISTS

**EDITED AND WITH AN INTRODUCTION
BY HAROLD BLOOM**

Printed and bound in the United States of America.

3 5 7 9 8 6 4 2

Library of Congress Cataloging-in-Publication Data
Alice Walker / edited and with an introduction by Harold Bloom.
p.   cm.—(Bloom's major novelists)
Includes bibliographical references (p.   ) and index.
ISBN 0-7910-5250-8 (hc)
1. Walker, Alice, 1944–   —Examination Study guides.   2. Women and literature—United States—History—20th century.   3. Afro–American in literature.
I. Bloom, Harold.   II. Series.
PS3573.A425Z535   1999
813'.54—dc21   99-14577
                                                         CIP

Chelsea House Publishers
1974 Sproul Road, Suite 400
Broomall, PA 19008-0914

The Chelsea House world wide web
address is www.chelseahouse.com

Contributing Editor: Tenley Williams

Contents

User's Guide

This volume is designed to present biographical, critical, and bibliographical information on the author's best-known or most important works. Following Harold Bloom's editor's note and introduction is a detailed biography of the author, discussing major life events and important literary accomplishments. A plot summary of each novel follows, tracing significant themes, patterns, and motifs in the work.

A selection of critical extracts, derived from previously published material from leading critics, analyzes aspects of each work. The extracts consist of statements from the author, if available, early reviews of the work, and later evaluations up to the present. A bibliography of the author's writings (including a complete list of all works written, cowritten, edited, and translated), a list of additional books and articles on the author and his or her work, and an index of themes and ideas in the author's writings conclude the volume.

Harold Bloom is Sterling Professor of the Humanities at Yale University and Henry W. and Albert A. Berg Professor of English at the New York University Graduate School. He is the author of over 20 books and the editor of more than 30 anthologies of literary criticism.

Professor Bloom's works include *Shelley's Mythmaking* (1959), *The Visionary Company* (1961), *Blake's Apocalypse* (1963), *Yeats* (1970), *A Map of Misreading* (1975), *Kabbalah and Criticism* (1975), and *Agon: Toward a Theory of Revisionism* (1982). *The Anxiety of Influence* (1973) sets forth Professor Bloom's provocative theory of the literary relationships between the great writers and their predecessors. His most recent books include *The American Religion* (1992), *The Western Canon* (1994), *Omens of Millennium: The Gnosis of Angels, Dreams, and Resurrection* (1996), and *Shakespeare: The Invention of the Human* (1998), a finalist for the 1998 National Book Award.

Professor Bloom earned his Ph.D. from Yale University in 1955 and has served on the Yale faculty since then. He is a 1985 MacArthur Foundation Award recipient, served as the Charles Eliot Norton Professor of Poetry at Harvard University in 1987–88, and has received honorary degrees from the universities of Rome and Bologna. In 1999, Professor Bloom received the prestigious American Academy of Arts and Letters Gold Medal for Criticism.

Currently, Harold Bloom is the editor of numerous Chelsea House volumes of literary criticism, including the series BLOOM'S NOTES, BLOOM'S MAJOR SHORT STORY WRITERS, BLOOM'S MAJOR POETS, MAJOR LITERARY CHARACTERS, MODERN CRITICAL VIEWS, MODERN CRITICAL INTERPRETATIONS, and WOMEN WRITERS OF ENGLISH AND THEIR WORKS.

Editor's Note

The Critical Extracts in this volume represent the principal critics, to date, of *Meridian* and *The Color Purple*. Marge Piercy and Susan Willis, ideological comrades of Walker, fiercely defend *Meridian*, as do the more scholarly Michael G. Cooke and John F. Callahan.

Gloria Steinem remains the most famous champion of *The Color Purple,* but receives support here from George Stade and Gerald Early. Darryl Pickney allows himself a few reservations, but these are set aside by the exemplary ferocity of Bell Hooks.

Introduction

HAROLD BLOOM

Whether Alice Walker will prove to be a period writer, intense though strident, or a permanent figure in American literature remains for time's revenges to clarify. *Meridian* and *The Color Purple*, rather like Toni Morrison's *Beloved*, are very much texts of our moment. Even a quick glance at the Critical Extracts presented in this brief volume will expose the reader to "saintly progress," "the Just person," "race and gender roles," "sexual justice," "the myth of Black Motherhood," "the idea of Revolution," "the American Dream," "ideological failure," and "the Erotic Metaphysic." The work of the novelist is to engross by storytelling, and by character development; to enhance or represent reality. Alice Walker is neither primarily a storyteller nor a representer of reality.

Meridian Hill, Walker's prime protagonist, is at the least a very considerable period piece. She is a martyr to the resistance to violence, a call she perpetually rejects. Like Lazarus, she is raised from the death of interracial strife, and what might be called interracial sexuality of the programmatic kind founded upon guilt and sorrow.

One can observe that Meridian Hill is an ideogram and not a person. Her lover, Truman Held, may be a travesty of the black male revolutionary, or he may be the thing itself. Either way, he is repugnant, evidently by design. After more than twenty years, Truman is not very persuasive, but then neither is Meridian Hill, nor her novel.

The Color Purple gave rather more to storytelling and less to ideology, but it also now seems a period-piece, furniture of the spirit. Poor Celie is everyone's victim, always being raped, beaten, or otherwise brutalized. Though Gloria Steinem found this "irresistible to read," less ideological readers may disagree. Alice Walker has intense pride and an authentic sense of social injustice. Whether these are, in themselves, aesthetic values remains open to considerable question. ❀

Biography of
Alice Walker

Alice Walker was born on February 9, 1944, in Eatonton, Georgia, the eighth and last child of Willie Lee and Minnie Tallulah Grant Walker. Her parents were tenant farmers, and the family endured the oppression of the sharecropping system and witnessed many incidents of violent racism. Walker was injured at age eight when her brother accidentally shot her with a BB gun. As a result of the accident, she lost sight in one eye. Thick scar tissue grew over the injured eye and she was warned that she might lose sight in the other eye. Perhaps as a result of her disfigurement and the isolation it imposed upon her, Walker spent her time reading and writing. In the close company of her mother and her aunts, she observed and drew upon the strength of independent women to shape her artistic vision. When she was fourteen, the scar tissue was removed.

Walker entered Spelman College, a college for black women in Atlanta, Georgia, in 1961, where she became involved in the civil rights movement. She transferred to Sarah Lawrence College two years later, and, after undergoing an abortion, she began writing the poems that would later be collected in her first published volume, *Once*. Walker graduated with a B.A. in 1965 and moved to New York's Lower East Side, where she worked for the Welfare Department. Soon thereafter, she moved to Mississippi where she became active in the civil rights movement. In 1966 Walker was a Breadloaf Writer's Conference Scholar and in 1967 received both a Merrill Writing Fellowship and a McDowell Colony Fellowship. On March 17, 1967, Walker married civil rights lawyer Melvyn Rosenman Leventhal; they worked together in Mississippi registering blacks to vote. Their daughter, Rebecca, was born before they divorced in 1976.

In 1968, Walker's first book of poetry, *Once,* was published; also that year she became writer-in-residence and teacher of black studies at Jackson State University, in Mississippi. The following year she taught at Tougaloo College. Her first novel, *The Third Life of Grange Copeland,* appeared in 1970. This straightforward narrative about three generations in the life of a black sharecropping family was praised for the sensitivity of its characterizations but received little popular or critical attention. In 1971 Walker received a Radcliffe Institute Fellowship and, while still on the Fellowship in 1972, taught literature at both Wellesley College and the University of Massachusetts. In 1973 her book of poems, *Revolutionary Petunias,* was published and received a National Book Award. The same year Walker received the Lillian Smith Award from the Southern Regional Council. *In Love and Trouble,* a collection of stories, was also published in 1973 and received the Rosenthal Foundation Award from the American Academy of Arts and Letters in 1974. *Langston Hughes: American Poet,* a biography written for children, was published in 1974. Walker became a contributing editor to *Ms.* magazine in 1975. The year 1976 marked Walker's divorce from Leventhal and the publication of her second novel, *Meridian,* considered by many to be the best novel of the civil rights era. In this novel Walker explores a woman's struggle to find a place in the civil rights movement; it also attacks sexism in African-American relationships. In an era when the civil rights movement was struggling to unify itself and to affirm its gains against racism, Walker's stance was controversial.

Walker received a Guggenheim Fellowship and her second McDowell Colony Fellowship in 1977. In 1979 she edited *I Love Myself When I Am Laughing . . . : A Zora Neale Hurston Reader* and published another volume of poems, *Good Night, Willie Lee, I'll See You in the Morning.* During this time she moved to California to write her next novel. *You Can't Keep a Good Woman Down,* a collection of stories, appeared in 1981. In 1982, the publication of *The Color Purple,* an epistolary bildungsroman about a southern black woman in oppressive, brutish circumstances, moved Walker into popular and critical success. This best-seller was nominated for a 1982 National Book Critics Circle Award, received the 1983 Pulitzer Prize and the American Book Award, and was made into an Academy Award–nominated film in 1985.

Alice Walker was named a distinguished writer in Afro-American Studies at the University of California at Berkeley in 1992. That spring she taught literature at Brandeis University as the Fannie Hurst Professor of Literature. In 1983 Walker published a book of "womanist" prose, *In Search of Our Mothers' Gardens.* Another book of poems, *Horses Make a Landscape More Beautiful,* appeared in 1984, and a volume of essays, *Living By the Word,* in 1988. Her most recent works include a volume of poetry, *Her Blue Body Everything*

We Know (1991), and two novels, *The Temple of My Familiar* (1989), about the reincarnation of an ancient African Goddess, and *Possessing the Secret of Joy* (1992), about a young woman who faces the African rite of circumcision.

Alice Walker's works have received considerable praise, particularly from the black and feminist communities. Her novels, poems, and essays often focus upon issues faced by black women struggling for racial and sexual equality. Though many have criticized her negative portraits of black men, in Alice Walker's works women emerge as strong and resourceful individuals who achieve selfhood in an emotional and intellectual community with other women. ❀

Plot Summary of
Meridian

Meridian, Alice Walker's second novel, is set against the civil rights movement and the call to militancy among young, college-educated, black Americans in the South. The protagonist, Meridian Hill, commits her life to the cause of black political and social equality. Divided into three sections, **Meridian, Truman Held**, and **Ending**, each with unnumbered chapters, the narrative explores issues of racism, sexual politics, and traditional African-American values during the social and political upheaval of the 1960s. In the first chapter, **The Last Return**, we are introduced to Meridian Hill through the eyes of her one-time lover, Truman Held, who has come from New York City to the southern town of Chicokema, Georgia, to see her. Ten years have passed since Meridian has been in New York. Truman watches, astonished, as Meridian, leading a group of schoolchildren, faces down an old army tank so that the children may view a freak show open to blacks only on Thursdays. The tank had "been bought during the sixties when the townspeople who were white felt under attack from 'outside agitators'—those members of the black community who thought equal rights for all should extend to blacks. They had painted it white, decked it with ribbons (red, white, and of course blue) and parked it in the public square." Truman is surprised that the civil rights movement hadn't changed all this.

Meridian suffers from some sort of wasting disease—or is it psychosomatic? We are never sure. Intermittent paralysis and fainting are accompanied by weight loss, bad skin, and eyes that are "glassy and yellow and [do] not seem to focus at once." But Meridian holds onto "something the others had let go," the African-American community that had existed before the revolutionary call to violence that she had resisted, bringing upon herself the scorn of her black militant friends. The purity of the songs in church reminds her of something even more essential than the political: "If they committed murder—and to her even revolutionary murder was murder—*what would the music be like?*" The novel revolves around this resistance to violence with comparisons of Meridian's commitment to the martyrs to the cause of civil rights, both black and white, such as Medgar Evers, Martin Luther King, Che Guevara, and Viola Liuzzo:

"Funerals became engraved on the brain, intensifying the ephemeral nature of life."

At Saxon College (**chapters two** and **three**), Meridian makes a futile attempt to rescue the pregnant and savage "Wile Chile" and witnesses the senseless destruction of the ancient "music" tree, called Sojourner, by the students rioting after their plan to eulogize the dead girl in the school's chapel is thwarted. Meridian's relationship with her parents is developed in **chapters four** through **six**. The depth of her mother's disappointments in life is measured by the question always asked when, as a child, Meridian would mention her own puzzling feelings of guilt. "Have you stolen anything?" her mother would respond. It seems that by her birth, Meridian had "stolen" her mother's future: "The question literally stopped her in her tracks." Her father, looking for "the historical vision of himself," researched the grim history of the local Indians, perhaps to gain a measure of detachment by which to come to some kind of terms with the history of his own people in America.

In **chapters seven** through **nine** Meridian, still in high school, discovers sex, marriage, motherhood, and the dissatisfactions commonly inherent in all three. A character portrait of her mother (**chapter ten**) reveals the impossibility of the older woman's own movement into political action. Overarching these issues is the deadly bombing of a house used for a black voter registration drive. This event turns Meridian's life toward the political: "And so it was that one day in the middle of April in 1960 Meridian Hill became aware of the past and present of the larger world." She volunteers at the voter registration office and meets the effete, charming, and politically committed Truman Held, "the first of the Civil Rights workers . . . who began to mean something to her." Against the backdrop of hypocrisy between lovers, Walker also explores, in Truman, the hypocrisy of some black nationalists (**chapters twelve** through **fourteen**). Meridian becomes pregnant and undergoes an abortion without telling Truman. Truman, in turn, has resumed a sexual relationship with a white "exchange student" and civil rights activist, Lynne Rabinowitz, a woman Meridian had liked. In an ugly moment, Truman attempts to win Meridian back to him: "You're *beautiful*," he whispered worshipfully. . . . "*Have* my beautiful black babies." She hits him, drawing blood. Her symptoms of paralysis and debilitation begin in **chapter fifteen**.

The second section of the novel, entitled **Truman Held**, examines issues of sexual politics through the lens of racism. Lynne views the black people of the South as Art. Two years after the infamous 1964 deaths of three civil rights workers, Truman and Lynne come to Mississippi: "If Mississippi is the worst place in America for black people, it stood to reason, [Lynne] thought, that the Art that was their lives would flourish best there." Truman for his part would rather live in France, but "wryly consider[s] Mississippi a just alternative" (**chapter sixteen**). Walker ruthlessly exposes the ugliness of interracial hatreds in the relationships of lovers and friends in **chapters seventeen** through **twenty-three**. Although Truman loves Lynne and they marry, he is forced to change his thinking on the issue of civil rights from an essentially race-blind assumption of equality back to the harsh reality of racism when his friend, Tommy Odds, lashes out at her as just one more of the hated race that shot him: "By being white Lynne was guilty of whiteness. . . . Then the question was, is it possible to be guilty of a color? Of course black people for years were 'guilty' of being black. Slavery was punishment for their 'crime.' . . . For bad or worse, and regardless of what this said about himself as a person he could not—after his friend's words— keep from thinking Lynne was, in fact guilty. The thing was to find out how." He never does: The question reveals that the essential absurdity of racism may be revealed without affecting it in the least. Lynne, always active in the movement, is increasingly ostracized. Truman, despite being her husband, is expected to discuss nothing of their activities with her. As the black militants gain power and confidence, their hatreds, like those of the whites, are strengthened and legitimized by racism.

Truman visits Meridian (**chapter eighteen**) and begs her "to give him another chance. She loved him, he rashly assumed—as she smiled at him—and he did not see why she should deny herself." Meridian is unimpressed; she will not betray her friendship with Lynne. She reminds him that he may "owe something" to his and Lynne's daughter, Camara. Truman is "stunned to learn that [Meridian] had long ago dismissed him. . . . For the first time he detected a quality in Meridian that Lynne . . . had insisted anyone could see. Meridian, no matter what she was saying to you . . . seemed to be thinking of something else, another conversation perhaps, an earlier one, that continued on a parallel track." She reminds him of his priggish demand for a virgin wife and he admits to himself that, when he had learned of the existence of Meridian's son, he had wondered only, "How could he have a wife who already had a child? And that she had given that child away. . . . When he knew about the child he thought of her breasts as used jugs. They had belonged to some other man."

Tommy Odds rapes Lynne in **chapter twenty-two**. But, he thinks, it isn't rape because she "had not screamed once, or even struggled very much." But, to Lynne this "was worse than rape because she felt circumstances had not permitted her to scream. . . . She lay instead thinking of his feelings, his hardships, of the way he was black and belonged to people who lived without hope; she thought about the loss of his arm. She felt her own guilt." When Truman later confronts him, Tommy Odds tells him "Black men get preferential treatment, man, to make up for all we been denied. She ain't been fucking you, she's been atoning for her sins." In response, Lynne seems to lose mental strength, and her affection for her black men friends at the center of the movement turns into sexual promiscuity. She deludes herself that her sexual relationships came "from love, not from hatred. For as long as they did not hate she felt she could live." She becomes pregnant, moves to New York City with Camara, and "magnanimously" sends Truman "back to Meridian, at his insistence." When six-year-old Camara is beaten to death, Truman and Lynne both turn to Meridian (**chapters twenty-three** and **twenty-four**): "It was Meridian they both needed, and it was Meridian who was, miraculously, there." Truman's roots are in the South, among the poor black community, but so are Lynne's, if not from childhood, from her love for Truman and her commitment, in youth, to the movement.

Lynn thinks back to her decision to come to the South (**chapter twenty-five**) and remembers the Jews who, like her, had come from New York and then had opened a delicatessen. They had been "shocked" and "aghast" when the local synagogue was bombed: "She laughed at their naivete. Laughed at their precarious 'safety.' Laughed with such bitter contempt that she could not speak to a Southern Jew without wanting to hit him or her." She returns to the present and remarks to Meridian, "Black folks aren't so special." Meridian replies, as if reading her mind, "Jews are fighting for Israel with one hand stuck in a crack in the Wailing Wall. Look at it this way, black folks and Jews held out as long as they could."

The last section of the novel, **Ending,** throws into sharp relief the legacy of racism against the struggle between militancy and peaceful protest. Walker does not turn from the complexity of the choice. We observe the funeral of Martin Luther King through Meridian's eyes in snapshot-like impressions, among the "crowd of nobodies who hungered to be nearer" (**chapter twenty-six**). But their somber song turns to idle chatter, laughter, and the ordinary; on a poodle's back a purple placard with white lettering proclaimed "I have a dream." "Meridian turned, in shame, as if to the dead man himself." In **chapter twenty-seven** Truman and Meridian continue their argument over the path to civil rights: He thinks revolution is an American fad; she asks, "Don't you think people, somewhere deep inside, are still attempting to deal with [the questions raised by King and Malcolm X]?" "No," he responds. The struggle, to Truman, is useless. He sees Meridian as a would-be martyr: "Why not go all out," he suggests, "and put rocks in your shoes?"

Meridian discovers in **chapter twenty-eight** that "Only in a church surrounded by the righteous guardians of the people's memories could she even approach the concept of retaliatory murder. Only among the pious could this idea both comfort and uplift." She understands clearly that she "does not belong to the future," but to "the old music" that is "the song of the people, transformed by the experiences of each generation." If she can carry this song forward, she thinks, her "role will not have been a useless one after all." This is countered—and balanced—with the rage she feels when confronted by the sight of a starving child or an adult who can neither read nor write. The song and the rage may yet be sufficient to "bring the mightiest country to its knees."

Chapters twenty-nine and **thirty** are comical vignettes of the task of voter registration. In **chapter thirty-one** Meridian and Truman "go to the prison. And so they must. And so they must see the child who murdered her child, nothing new." They have registered her mother and sister to vote and have come to visit this 13-year-old girl who had strangled her baby, her "heart." "And why am I alive, without my heart?" she asks. They leave her; it "was too much for them." Meridian expects to feel something for the son she had given up but feels something only for the "doomed" girl with the "heart of stone." Truman, however, "lay as if slaughtered, feeling a warmth, as of hot blood, wash over him. Shame. But for what? For whom? What had he done?" In **chapters thirty-two** and **thirty-three** Truman attempts to answer these questions, without much success. Meridian, however, seems to have gained spiritual and physical strength by the final chapter. To Truman, she seems like Lazarus: "Meridian would return to the world cleansed of sickness." ❁

List of Characters in
Meridian

Meridian Hill is the protagonist of the novel. She is a college-educated young woman who commits herself to the cause of civil rights among the black community in the South during the 1960s. She joins a voter registration project that evolves into a black militant organization she is forced to leave when she cannot agree that the capacity to kill is necessary to the achievement of equality and social justice. She is nonetheless a committed political activist. Her struggle throughout the novel is to reconcile the hypocrisy, racism, and violence of black nationalism with the spirituality, compassion, and fierce commitment of the legacy of Martin Luther King, Malcolm X, and the songs that tell the black history.

Truman Held is Meridian's lover and also an activist in the civil rights movement working to register black Southerners to vote. Charming, educated, and effete, he struggles to come to terms with the love he has for the aesthetic beauty of the black woman with the stereotypical, but nonetheless powerful, attraction to white women. While Truman often seems both hypocritical and committed more to his own self-interest than to black causes, he attempts to reconcile the ugliest and most bitter aspects of racial and sexual conflicts.

Lynne Rabinowitz comes to the South during the civil rights movement of the early 1960s and participates in the drive to register black voters. She marries Truman Held and their daughter, Camara, is beaten and killed, at age six, in New York City. Her friendship with Meridian grows and endures even Truman's return to Meridian. ❁

Critical Views on
Meridian

MARGE PIERCY ON MERIDIAN'S SAINTLY PROGRESS

[Marge Piercy is a novelist, poet, and teacher. Her works include *Woman on the Edge of Time* (1977), *Fly Away Home* (1985), and *City of Darkness, City of Light* (1996). The review of *Meridian* that the following excerpt is taken from originally appeared in the *New York Times Book Review* in May 1976.]

In *Meridian*, Alice Walker has written a fine, taut novel that accomplishes a remarkable amount. The issues she is concerned with are massive. Events are strung over 25 years, although most occur between the height of the civil rights movement and the present. However, her method of compression through selection of telling moments and her freedom from chronology create a lean book that ⟨. . .⟩ goes down like clean water. ⟨. . .⟩

She writes with a sharp critical sense as she deals with the issues of tactics and strategy in the civil rights movement, with the nature of commitment, the possibility of interracial love and communication, the vital and lethal strands in American and black experience, with violence and nonviolence, holiness and self-hatred. ⟨. . .⟩

Meridian, the protagonist, is the most interesting [character in the book], an attempt to make real in contemporary terms the notion of holiness and commitment. Is it possible to write a novel about the progress of a saint? Apparently, yes. With great skill and care to make Meridian believable at every stage of her development, Walker also shows us the cost. For every exemplary act of bravery for the black community (standing up to a tank so black children can see a peepshow) she pays an immediate price in her body. Asked by a group of temporary revolutionaries if she can kill for the revolution, she infuriates her friends because she cannot say an easy yes and spends a decade worrying the question.

Walker has put Meridian together carefully, on every level.

I do not find the ending successful. Walker consciously rejects death. Meridian's political commitment is not to end in martyrdom:

there have been too many martyrs to her cause. Still, we need some other equivalent of death or marriage to round off a tale, and Walker has not found one here. We are told that Meridian has brought off a successful change from victim to fully responsible protagonist. . . . But telling is not enough. She has ceased to be one sort of committed person and become another. Some act is needed to make real the change and it isn't there; but that's a minor failure in a tight, fascinating novel.

—Marge Piercy, Review of *Meridian* in the *New York Times Book Review* (23 May 1976): pp. 135–136.

THE *NEW YORKER* ON THE PHILOSOPHY OF *MERIDIAN*

[This excerpt is from an unsigned review of Alice Walker's *Meridian* that appeared in the *New Yorker* on June 7, 1976. It discusses the "down-to-earth" philosophy of the novel.]

At its best, . . . the tone of [*Meridian* is] flat, direct, measured, deliberate, with a distinct lack of drama. . . . And the tone is right; it's not the plot that carries the novel forward but Meridian's attempt to resolve, or preserve the reality of, the questions of knowledge, history, and murder that Miss Walker introduces early on. The astonishing dramatic intensity that Walker brought to *The Third Life of Grange Copeland* would in *Meridian* blow those questions apart.

But such questions lead all too easily to high-flown language and to pretensions that fictional characters cannot support, which is why most "philosophical" novels are impossible to reread. Miss Walker does not always avoid this trap; though her tendency is to insist on the prosaic, to bring philosophy down to earth, Meridian at times seems to be floating straight to Heaven. The book tries to make itself a parable—more than a mere novel—or trades the prosaic for an inert symbolism that would seem to be intended to elevate the story but instead collapses it. ⟨. . .⟩

Meridian is interesting enough without ⟨. . .⟩ symbolism and "higher meanings" that are one-dimensional and fixed. There is no mystery in these symbols ⟨. . .⟩ and a symbol without mystery, without suggestive power, is not really a symbol at all. But most of the book's scenes have the power its symbols lack, and its last chapters rescue Meridian's questions from a holy oblivion. For they are resolved, after a fashion, and passed on . . . not only to the book's other characters, who share Meridian's life, but perhaps to the reader as well.

—Review of the novel in *New Yorker* (7 June 1976): p. 208.

MICHAEL G. COOKE ON WALKER'S VISION OF THE JUST PERSON

[Michael G. Cooke has written numerous articles on Alice Walker. This essay, which originally appeared in the *Yale Review,* discusses the character of Meridian.]

⟨Alice Walker⟩ deals, in *Meridian*, with a heroine who has not fully broken the gravitational field of the '60's; if she keeps the faith, as most do not, she also feels the fetters of the disbanded revolutionary movement, as most do not. Prematurely aged, preternaturally reflective in the continual hot demand for justice and self-fulfillment— still the two great passions of our time—Meridian must decide whether she will, for the cause, commit the ultimate violence of killing. The problem is that she considers this the ultimate violence to herself as well as to another. The book is a patchwork of incidents, memories, projections, with a continual sense of performance, of ritual acts and even thoughts for public consumption and assay. Meridian's name echoes ritually in those of other female characters, Anne and Anne-Marion. It echoes even more tellingly in the high-noon quality of the situations in which so many of the characters find themselves—stark, boundary-marking situations concerning the very choice of life they must make. Some will hear echoes of *The Autobiography of Miss Jane Pittman* here, but Walker's work is far more inward, and more socially complex withal, than Gaines's. The culminating scene of the defiant old lady in *Miss Jane Pittman* is the opening scene of *Meridian*, as if Walker were moving on from Gaines as deliberately as Wordsworth from Milton.

Oates contends à la Skinner that "the personal life is over," but Alice Walker has her version of the eternal "wanderer . . . looking for . . . anything to keep his historical vision of himself as a just person from falling apart."

A vision of the just person, rather than of the right-on revolutionary or the now-or-never woman, informs *Meridian*.

More than ordinary action, violence is transitory and exhausts its resources and its goals. What Walker slowly appreciates through Meridian is the enormous energies composed in true, choice inaction, the great questions resolved in the endless debate of silence. The fruitfulness of Meridian's choice of inaction and silence may be revealed in the growing back of her hair, in her rejuvenation and refeminization. It is a choice less synecdochic (one woman for all) than paradigmatic (every woman must decline, parse by herself).

—Michael G. Cooke, "A Vision of the Just Person in *Meridian*," *Yale Review* (Autumn 1976): p. 155.

PETER ERICKSON ON THE RELATIONSHIP BETWEEN MOTHER AND DAUGHTER

[Peter Erickson is professor of English at the Clark Institute of Art. His works include *The Stance of Atlas: An Examination of the Philosophy of Ayn Rand* (1997), *Patriarchal Studies in Shakespeare's Drama* (1985), and he is editor, with Coppelia Kahn, of *Shakespeare's "Rough Magic"* (1985). Erickson discusses Meridian's relationship with her mother in this essay.]

The exploration of the relationship between Meridian and her mother is an instance of Alice Walker's ruminative style. A meandering, yet disciplined, meditation is effected by continually dropping the subject and later returning to it for a fresh look; intricacy and intensity are built up by this circling back to take up another facet of the mother-daughter relationship, to press the analysis further. Walker establishes a frame of reference in the present from which she can delve into the past. Meridian's mother is introduced in a flashback within a flashback as "that past" which cannot be ignored.

Meridian's troubled feelings about her mother revolve around the conflict between the need to love her mother—"it is death not to love one's mother"—and the need to be different from her. Meridian is unable to break away easily from her mother because "an almost primeval guilt" prevents her from criticizing her mother:

> She imagined her mother in church, in which she had invested all that was still energetic in her life, praying for her daughter's soul, and yet, having no concern, no understanding of her daughter's *life* whatsoever; but Meridian did not condemn her for this.

> To Meridian, her mother *was* a giant. . . . That her mother was deliberately obtuse about what had happened meant nothing beside her own feelings of inadequacy and guilt. Besides, she had already forgiven her mother for anything she had ever done to her or might do.

> It seemed to Meridian that her legacy from her mother's endurance . . . was one she would never be able to match. It never occurred to her that her mother's and her grandmother's extreme purity of life was compelled by necessity. They had not lived in an age of choice.

The lives of mother and daughter are similar in that the crucial event is pregnancy. As Meridian perceives it, her mother "could never forgive her community, her family, the whole world, for not warning her against children." By her existence, Meridian spoils her mother's life: "It was for stealing her mother's serenity, for shattering her mother's emerging self, that Meridian felt guilty from the very first." Meridian's own pregnancy—for which her mother had not prepared her—"came as a total shock" and compounds her guilt. After her husband abandons her, she has an opportunity to go to college, which she is unwilling to give up. To pursue her education, she decides to give away her child despite the opposition of her mother: "'I have six children,' she continued self-righteously, 'though I never wanted to have any, and I have raised every one myself.'" Meridian follows the courage of her conviction, but her mother's disapproval takes its toll: "[S]he felt condemned, consigned to penitence, for life. . . . She thought of her mother as being worthy of this maternal history, and of herself as belonging to an unworthy minority." A second pregnancy, about which Meridian confides to no one, is ended by abortion. In the culminating chapter of this first part (entitled "Meridian"), a teacher at Saxon College grants Meridian the forgiveness she would like to have received from her mother: "Instictively, as if Meridian were her own child, Miss Winter answered, close to her ear on the pillow, 'I forgive you.'" Ultimately Meridian extends this forgiveness to Truman Held: "know i wish to forgive you" (compare Ruth's "unforgiveness" toward Brownfield).

A chapter later in the novel ("Camara") involves a reconsideration of two issues posed in the very first chapter—Meridian's inability to commit herself either to revolutionary violence or to the church. She is now caught by surprise by the church's reorientation:

> And what was Meridian, who had always thought of the black church as mainly a reactionary power, to make of this? . . . Perhaps it was, after all, the only place left for black people to congregate, where the problems of life were not discussed fraudulently and the approach to the future was considered communally, and moral questions were taken seriously.

In Meridian's rediscovery of the church, there is perhaps an implicit reconciliation with her mother. In seeing the church (which had originally divided mother and daughter) as a positive force, Meridian accepts a legacy—however transformed—of her mother. Through her experience of the church, Meridian envisions herself as an artist:

> [P]erhaps it will be my part to walk behind the real revolutionaries—those who know they must spill blood in order to help the poor and the black and therefore go right ahead and when they stop to wash off the blood and find their throats too choked with the smell of murdered flesh to sing, I will come forward and sing from memory songs they will need once more to hear. For it is the song of the people, transformed by the experience of each generation, that holds them together, and if any part of it is lost the people suffer and are without soul. If I can only do that, my role will not have been a useless one after all.

Though Meridian remains apart, she retains the religious feeling of "communal spirit, togetherness, righteous convergence." It is this sense of relatedness which qualifies her isolation at the hymn-like end of the novel: "[A]ll the people who are as alone as I am will one day gather at the river. We will watch the evening sun go down. And in the darkness maybe we will know the truth."

—Peter Erickson, "'Cast Out Alone/to Heal/and Re-Create Our-selves': Family-Based Identity in the Work of Alice Walker," *CLA Journal* 23, no. 1 (September 1979). Reprinted in *Alice Walker*, ed. Harold Bloom (New York: Chelsea House, 1989): pp. 21–23.

DEBORAH E. MCDOWELL ON RACE AND GENDER ROLES

[Deborah E. McDowell is professor of English and African-American Studies at the University of Virginia. She is author of *The Changing Same: Studies in Fiction by Black Women* (1994) and *Slavery and the Literary Imagination* (1988). In this essay McDowell discusses the way that Meridian challenges traditional race and gender roles in her search for self-discovery.]

One of the most perpetually looming obstacles to Meridian's struggle for self-discovery is the god of American tradition. But rather than cower and defer to its menacing force, she confronts it. Whether represented by people, institutions, established "truths," or time-worn abstractions, Meridian examines tradition with a critical eye and rejects those aspects which impinge upon her self-discovery.

That much of Meridian's growth process will entail a confrontation with the god of tradition, or the "dead hand" of the past, is established in the richly symbolic, tightly compressed opening chapter in which two of America's most cherished institutions—racism and sexism—meet head-on in a skillful, simultaneous dramatization. The chapter recounts the circus show, conducted Jim Crow style, featuring the mummy woman, Marilene O'Shay, "one of the Twelve Wonders of the World: Preserved in Life-Like Condition."

At the most fundamental level, Walker is satirizing the tenacious but untenable belief in tradition, which is at the bowels of American culture, for the preservation of the mummy woman is a metaphor for the preservation of dead, no longer viable traditions and institutions. Thus Meridian challenges this Southern town's "separate-but-equal" racial tradition by leading a group of black school children to the circus wagon on a day not authorized by the local government.

While defying the tradition of separate-but-equal race relations, Meridian, in her active social role, concurrently challenges traditional and synthetic images of women. She is in sharp contradistinction to the images presented of the mummy woman (which are, Walker suggests, images of all women). The marquee of the circus wagon flashes the captions "Obedient Daughter," "Devoted Wife" and "Adoring Mother," the traditional stages of a woman's life. The circus bill (significantly written by the mummy woman's husband) explains that she had been "an ideal woman," a "goddess," who had been given "everythin," that is, "a washing machine, furs, her own car and a full-time housekeeper cook." Her only duty was to "lay back and be pleasured." But the mummy woman loses her fringe benefits and her life in the process. Her husband kills her because she "had gone outside the home to seek her 'pleasuring,' while still expecting him to foot the bills." This image of woman as passivist, as "a mindless body, a sex creature, something to hang false hair and nails on," is actively challenged by Meridian in her role as a human rights crusader. It is not incidental that her physical features in this chapter most resemble a male's. Most of her hair has fallen out and she wears an old railroad cap and dungarees which have masculine suggestions. But the fact that she is physically unattractive does not concern Meridian, an unconcern contrary to conventional notions of womanhood. Not only does Meridian look like a male, but she also acts like one. She is decidedly out of her "place" as a woman in her demonstration of unwavering leadership qualities, those generally associated with the male. Although there are armed policemen stationed in a "red-white-and-blue" army tank to prevent Meridian from fulfilling her mission, she bravely marches on, facing the tank aimed at her chest. "The silence as Meridian kicked open the door, exploded in a mass exhalation of breaths, and the men who were in the tank crawled sheepishly out again to stare." Thus a symbolic inversion of roles occurs in this scene and Meridian can be said to triumph over tradition and authority. Her achievement in this series of attacks on tradition is a pointed commentary on America's role-dependency. She exemplifies Toni Cade's assertion that

> You find your Self in destroying illusions, smashing myths
> . . . being responsible to some truth, to the struggle. That
> entails . . . cracking through the veneer of this sick society's
> definition of 'masculine' and 'feminine'

and striving towards creating an androgynous, fluid self.

Such fluidity of personality is necessary because rigid role definitions are static; by their very nature, they deny human complexity and thereby stifle growth, completeness of being.

—Deborah E. McDowell, "The Self in Bloom: Alice Walker's *Meridian*," *CLA Journal* 19, no. 3 (March 1981): pp. 262–275.

CAROL RUMENS ON RACIAL EQUALITY AND SEXUAL JUSTICE

[Carol Rumens is a British poet and critic. She is editor of *New Women Poets* (1991) and author of several books of poetry, including *Thinking of Skins, Best China Sky* (1994), and *From Heaven to Berlin* (1990). In this essay she compares *Meridian* to Walker's book of short stories *You Can't Keep a Good Woman Down* (1981).]

⟨Alice Walker's *Meridian* and *You Can't Keep a Good Woman Down*⟩ are difficult in that, to varying degrees, they presuppose a certain awareness on the part of their readers; they are also, at best, strong and passionately visionary pieces of prose with a quality of the epic poem. They are heirs to the dream of Martin Luther King, and are at the same time committed and coolly clearsighted concerning its progress. The feminism of ⟨Alice Walker⟩ is the source of ⟨her⟩ detachment; although the question of racial equality is primary, it is focussed through, and to some extent even diminished by, the often more urgently personal quest for sexual justice. ⟨. . .⟩ Her deepest concern is with individuals and how their relationships are affected by their confrontations with wider political and moral issues. The sexism inherent in historical racism and still beleaguering most attempts at honest radicalism is neatly teased out and laid bare.

Meridian is the most accessible of the books, and the most plural in its concerns. ⟨. . .⟩ The narrative itself is solidly constructed and makes powerful use of symbols in a manner reminiscent of Toni Morrison.

The short stories ⟨in⟩ *You Can't Keep a Good Woman Down* tend to be less subtly imagined. Often ruggedly open-ended in form, they suggest that Alice Walker is happier with a larger canvas. Some seem rather detached and essay-like. ⟨. . .⟩ In the best of them, as in *Meridian*, considerations of sexual and racial politics are resonant with universal moral overtones. There is the question posed by Luna, for example, a white sympathizer whose problem is "whether in a black community surrounded by whites with a history of lynching blacks, she had a right to scream as Freddie Pye was raping her." Walker has a particular gift for capturing the pathos of sexual love; it is the subject of "Laurel", a story of a black-white triangle in which colour, however, plays only a minimal part. ⟨. . .⟩ Walker's work should be admired ⟨. . .⟩ not because it represents a flowering of black or female consciousness, but because at best it brings to life the varied scents and colours of human experience.

—Carol Rumens, "Heirs to the Dream," *The Times Literary Supplement* (18 June 1982): p. 676.

THADIOUS M. DAVIS ON THE CREATION OF A PERSONAL IDENTITY

[Thadious M. Davis is Gertrude Conway Vanderbilt Professor of English at Vanderbilt University. She is author of *Faulkner's "Negro": Art and the Southern Context* (1983) and *Nella Larsen: A Woman's Life Unveiled* (1994), and co-editor, with Trudier Harris, of several books of criticism. In this extract, Davis compares family relationships in *Meridian* with Alice Walker's first novel, *The Third Life of Grange Copeland*.]

In ⟨Walker's⟩ first novel, *The Third Life of Grange Copeland,* three generations of Copelands converge to create Ruth's identity, and three generations form the stages or lives of the patriarch and title character, Grange Copeland. When any one member of the Copeland family or of a particular social generation of blacks (from 1920 to 1960) ignores the dynamics of family structures or forgets the historical perspective that the structures are maintained through necessity and love, he or she loses the capacity for primary identifications with race, family, and community, and loses as well the major basis for defining one's self and one's humanity. The most detailed illustration presented in the novel is Brownfield, the son of Grange and a member of the middle generation in the work.

Brownfield Copeland becomes one of "the living dead, one of the many who had lost their souls in the American wilderness." He reduces his murder of his wife to a simple therorem: "He *liked plump women. . . . Ergo,* he had murdered his wife because she had become skinny." Because of his twisted logic, Brownfield "could forget [his wife's] basic reality, convert it into comparisons. She had been like good pie, or good whiskey, but there had never been a self to her." Not only by means of the murder itself, but also by the process of his reasoning about it, he strips himself of his humanity when he negates his culpability with the negation of his wife's existence as a human being.

Brownfield's physical death sadly, though appropriately in Walker's construction, comes at the hands of his father Grange and over the future of his daughter Ruth. But his spiritual death occurs much earlier "as he lay thrashing about, knowing the rigidity of his belief in misery, knowing he could never renew or change himself, for this changelessness was now all he had, he could not clarify what was the duty of love." He compounds one of the greatest sins in Walker's works, the refusal or inability to change, with his dismissal of meaning in family bonds. Ironically, his death makes possible the completion of change in his daughter's life that had been fostered by his father, who late in his life understood the necessity of moving beyond the perverted emotions constricting the lives of the Copelands.

In *Meridian,* Walker's second novel, the heroine divests herself of immediate blood relations—her child and her parents—in order to align herself completely with the larger racial and social generations of blacks. Meridian Hill insists that although seemingly alone in the world, she has created a fusion with her generation of activist blacks and older generations of oppressed blacks. The form of the work, developed in flashbacks, follows a pattern of Meridian's casting off the demands made by authority and responsibility within the conventional family and traditional institutions. Unlike Brownfield's rejection of responsibility, the rupture in this novel is ultimately positive, despite its being the most radical and mysterious instance of change and acceptance in Walker's fiction. It is positive because the novel creates a new basis for defining Meridian's self and for accepting responsibility for one's actions. In fact, the controlling metaphor is resurrection and rebirth, an acting out of the renewal impossible for Brownfield. By the end of the novel, Meridian's personal identity has become a collective identity. "There is water in the world for us / brought by our friends," she writes in one of her two poems, "though the rock of mother and god / vanishes into sand / and we, cast out alone / to heal / and re-create / ourselves." In spite of her painful private experiences, Meridian is born anew into a pluralistic cultural self, a "we" that is and must be selfless and without ordinary prerequisites for personal identity. And significantly, because she exemplifies Walker's recurrent statement of women as leaders and models, Meridian leaves her male disciple Truman Held to follow her and to await the arrival of others from their social group.

Truman's search, structurally a duplication of Meridian's, is part of personal change that is more necessary for men than for women in Walker's fiction and that becomes social change through the consequences of actions taken by individuals who must face constraints, as well as opportunities, in their lives, but must also know why they act and what the consequences will be. Truman resolves to live the life of an ascetic so that he might one day be worthy to join Meridian and others "at the river," where they "will watch the evening sun go down. And in the darkness maybe [they] will know the truth." The search for truth leads Truman, like Meridian, to a commitment to the social generation of blacks to which he belongs. He follows Meridian's rationale for his action: "i want to put an end to guilt / i want to put an end to shame / whatever you have done my sister / (my brother) / know i wish to forgive you / love you." By so doing, Truman accepts his personal duty towards

all blacks, discovers his own meaning, and commits his life in love
to both present and future generations.

—Thadious M. Davis, "Walker's Celebration of Self in Southern Gen-
erations," *The Southern Quarterly* 21, no. 4 (Summer 1983).
Reprinted in *Alice Walker*, ed. Harold Bloom (New York: Chelsea
House, 1989): pp. 33–35.

BARBARA CHRISTIAN ON THE MYTH OF BLACK MOTHERHOOD

[Barbara Christian is professor of English and African-
American Studies at the University of California at Berkeley.
Her books include *Black Feminist Criticism* (1985) and
*Black Women Novelists: The Development of a Tradition,
1892–1976* (1980). In this extract, Christian opines that
Meridian challenges stereotypes, as well as restrictions, of
motherhood.]

⟨I⟩n *Meridian* she scrutinized that tradition which is based on the
monumental myth of black motherhood, a myth based on the true
stories of sacrifice black mothers performed for their children. But
the myth is also restrictive, for it imposes a stereotype of black
women, a stereotype of strength which denies them choice, and
hardly admits of the many who were destroyed. In her characterization of Margaret and Mem Copeland in *The Third Life of Grange
Copeland* Walker acknowledged the abused black women who,
unlike Faulkner's Dilsey, did not endure. She went a step further in
Meridian. Meridian's quest for wholeness and her involvement in
the Civil Rights movement is initiated by her feelings of inadequacy
in living up to the standards of black motherhood. Meridian gives
up her son because she believes she will poison his growth with the
thorns of guilt and she has her tubes tied after a painful abortion. In
this novel, then, Walker probed the idea of black motherhood, as she
developed a character who so elevates it that she at first believes she
can not properly fulfill it. Again, Walker approaches the forbidden as
a possible route to another truth.

Not only did Walker challenge the monument of black motherhood in *Meridian,* she also entered the fray about the efficacy of motherhood in which American feminists were then, as they now are, engaged. As many radical feminists blamed motherhood for the waste in women's lives and saw it as a dead end for a woman, Walker insisted on a deeper analysis: she did not present motherhood in itself as restrictive. It is so because of the little value society places on children, especially black children, on mothers, especially black mothers, on life itself. In the novel, Walker acknowledged that a mother in this society is often "buried alive, walled away from her own life, brick by brick." Yet the novel is based on Meridian's insistence on the sacredness of life. Throughout her quest she is surrounded by children whose lives she tries to preserve. In seeking the children she can no longer have she takes responsibility for the life of all the people. Her aborted motherhood yields to her a perspective on life—that of "expanding her mind with action." In keeping with this principle, Walker tells us in her essay "*One* Child of One's Own":

> It is not my child who has purged my face from history
> and herstory and left mystory just that, a mystery; my
> child loves my face and would have it on every page, if
> she could, as I have loved my own parents' faces above all
> others, and refused to let them be denied, or myself to let
> them go.

In fact, *Meridian* is based on this idea, the sacredness and continuity of life—and on another, that it might be necessary to take life in order to preserve it and make it possible for future generations. Perhaps the most difficult paradox that Walker has examined to date is the relationship between violence and revolution, a relationship that so many take for granted that such scrutiny seems outlandish. Like her heroine, Meridian, who holds on to the idea of nonviolent resistance after it has been discarded as a viable means to change, Walker persists in struggling with this age-old dilemma—that of death giving life. What the novel *Meridian* suggests is that unless such a struggle is taken on by those who would change society, their revolution will not be integral. For they may destroy that which they abhor only to resurrect it in themselves. Meridian discovers, only through personal struggle in conjunction with her involvement with the everyday lives of her people, that the respect she owed her life was to continue, against whatever obstacles, to live it, and not to give up any particle of it without a fight to the death, preferably *not* her own. And that this existence extended beyond herself to those around her because, in fact, the years in America had created them One Life.

But though the concept of One Life motivates Meridian in her quest toward physical and spiritual health, the societal evils which subordinate one class to another, one race to another, one sex to another, fragment and ultimately threaten life. So that the novel *Meridian*, like *The Third Life of Grange Copeland*, is built on the tension between the African concept of animism, "that spirit inhabits all life," and the societal forces that inhibit the growth of the living toward their natural state of freedom.

—Barbara Christian, "The Black Woman Artist as Wayward," *Black Women Writers (1950–1980)*, ed. Mari Evans (Garden City, N.Y.: Doubleday/Anchor, 1984): pp. 82–83.

Susan Willis on the Radical Potential of Language

[Susan Willis is associate professor of English and literature at Duke University. She is author of *A Primer for Daily Life* (1991), *The BBC Shakespeare Plays: Making the Televised Canon* (1991), and *Specifying: Black Women Writing the American Experience* (1989). In this extract, Willis discusses how Meridian's mystical experiences shape her efforts to bring about political change.]

Of the novels, *Meridian* offers the clearest view of the process of radicalization. For Meridian, the autobiographical embodiment of Walker herself, coming of age in the 1960s does not offer a free ticket but provides an atmosphere of confrontation and the questioning of contradiction with which the individual must grapple. Early in the book it becomes clear that one of the most profound ideologies to be confronted and transcended is the acceptance of mystical explanations for political realities. Meridian's childhood is steeped in Indian lore, the walls of her room papered with photographs of the great Indian leaders from Sitting Bull and Crazy Horse to the romanticized Hiawatha. Moreover, her father's farm includes an ancient Indian burial mound, its crest shaped like a serpent, where, in the coil of its tail, Meridian achieves a state of "ecstasy." Absorbed in a dizzying spin, she feels herself lifted out of her body while all around her—family and countryside—are caught up in the spinning whirlpool of her consciousness. It is not odd that Walker focuses on mystical experience. After all, this is a book about the 1960s whose counterculture opened the door to more than one form of mysticism. It is also not strange that Meridian's mystical experience derives from Native American culture given the long cohistorical relationship between blacks and Indians (in the southeastern United States) whose radical union goes back to the time of cimarrons and Seminoles.

However, ecstasy is not the answer. While Meridian will learn from the mystical experience, it will not be sufficient to her life's work to rely upon the practice of retreat into the ecstatic trance. What, then, of the historic link between Indians and blacks? If, in the course of the book, Meridian learns to transcend ecstasy, is this a denial of her (and her people's) relationship to the Indian people?

Definitely not: the book's preface gives us another way of defining Meridian's relationship to Native Americans, which the great lesson taught by her radicalization will bring into reality. Taken from *Black Elk Speaks,* this is the book's preface:

> I did not know then how much was ended. When I look back now . . . I can still see the butchered women and children lying heaped and scattered all along the crooked gulch as plain as when I saw them with eyes still young. And I can see that something else died there in the bloody mud, and was buried in the blizzard. A people's dream died there. It was a beautiful dream . . . the nation's hoop is broken and scattered. There is no center any longer, and the sacred tree is dead.

Black Elk's words remember the massacre of Wounded Knee which for Indian people was the brutal cancellation of their way of life. The dream Black Elk refers to is the vision he, as a holy man, had of his people and their world: "The leaves on the trees, the grasses on the hills and in the valleys, the waters in the creeks and in the rivers and the lakes, the four-legged and the two-legged and the wings of the air—all danced together to the music of the stallion's song."

This is a vision of a community of man and nature, which Black Elk, as a holy man, must bring into being—not individually, but through the collective practice of the group. As he sees it, the nation is a "hoop" and "Everything an Indian does is in a circle, and that is because the Power of the World always works in circles, and everything tries to be round." These are images of a community's wholeness, which Meridian takes as her political paradigm—not the particulars of Indian culture: not the beads which Hippies grafted on their white middle-class identities, not the swoons of ecstasy— but the Indian view of community, in which the holy man or seer is not marginal, but integral to the group. So when Meridian says she will "go back to the people," and when she leads them in demonstration against racists practices, she enacts Black Elk's formula for praxis. As an intellectual and a political activist, she understands that the individual's inspiration for social change can only be realized through the group's collective activity.

—Susan Willis, "Alice Walker's Women," *The New Orleans Review* 12, no. 1 (Spring 1985). Reprinted in *Alice Walker*, ed. Harold Bloom (New York: Chelsea House, 1989): pp. 89–90.

JOHN F. CALLAHAN ON THE IDEA OF REVOLUTION

[John F. Callahan is Morgan S. Odell Professor of Humanities at Lewis and Clark College. He is author of *In the African-American Grain: Call and Response in Twentieth-Century Black Fiction* (1990). In this essay, he discusses what Meridian is willing to do in order to create social change.]

Called back to the present "from a decidedly unrevolutionary past," Meridian struggles to overcome the paradoxical conflict between politics and personality. Her contemporaries, she realizes, "made her ashamed of the past, and yet all of them had shared it," whereas she keeps faith with the sustaining personal warmth of the past as a touchstone of contemporary politics. But she does not reject her comrades; "she felt she loved them," even though "love was not what they wanted, it was not what they needed." As she does with her mother (and also the young men who pursue her sexually), Meridian tries not to offend or alienate, even if she cannot please. Using the familiar pattern of call-and-response, she seeks common ground in the chaos and violence of American life. Slowly, she becomes the lead voice, and the others join her call believing she is about to announce her willingness to "kill for the Revolution":

> "I know I want what is best for black people."
> "That's what we all want!"
> "I know there must be a revolution. . . ."
> "Damn straight!"
> "I know violence *is* as American as cherry pie!"
> "Rap on!"
> "I know nonviolence has failed."

Meridian understands the struggle and the lingo. She has marched and been abused, beaten, and jailed, and she has gone back out on the line. She know how to speak *to* her contemporaries and *for* them—so much so that they answer her rhythmic, repetitive *I knows* with one voice.

Her words invoke the simplicities of the current situation, but her pause implies its complexities as well as her refusal to enter the country of false eloquence. But Meridian's audience rejects the intimate, contemplative note her brief silence brings to the dialogue. They seek capitulation from her, not conversation with her. But their failure to let her respond individually to the collective call—"Then you will kill for the Revolution, not just die for it?"—chases her back to the private region of her mind. "I don't know" she says, and her truthful answers to this and subsequent questions make her an outcast. She is the victim of psychological political aggression reminiscent of Janie Starks's wifely experience in *Their Eyes Were Watching God*: "Mah own mind had tuh be squeezed and crowded out tuh make room for yours in me." Yet Meridian is not entirely a casualty. When a former friend among the revolutionaries asks her condescendingly, "What will you do? Where will you go?" Meridian keeps faith with those images and voices that persist in the depths of her mind as companions to her identity:

> "I'll go back to the people, live among them like Civil
> Rights workers used to do."
> "You're not serious?"
> "Yes," she said. "I am serious."

Unlike the others, because of her past (and her self-restoring sense of *the* past), Meridian cannot even pretend to disconnect political work from personal experience, particularly her surrender of her child and the related loss of her mother as psychological kin. Now in a simple courageous voice Meridian tells this hostile audience her choice: a life and politics committed to love and creation instead of hate and violence. She still does not know definitely whether or not she should or could kill for the revolution or for any other cause. But she does know that her answer must be her people's answer, and she cannot discover either in New York. (In her glossary Walker gives *southern* as a rare meaning for meridian, and Meridian is the name of the Mississippi town in which the murdered black Civil Rights worker, James Cheney, grew up and was buried in 1964.) Like Jean Toomer who went to Georgia seeking a loving artistic voice, Meridian goes south in quest of a loving political voice, rooted in her life and the people's—what Robert Hayden, in his poem for Frederick Douglass, calls "this beautiful and terrible . . . needful thing" of freedom. But Meridian alters Hayden's idea of "lives grown out of [Douglass's] life" (*Angle of Ascent*). Her new life will grow from the people, provided she is able "to see them, to be with them, to understand them *and herself,*" while, true to her vision, they become next of kin "who now fed her and tolerated her and also, in a fashion, *cared* about her" (*Meridian,* my italics).

As Walker tells of Meridian's gradual personal revolution, her voice achieves a muted simplicity and eloquence. Her relationship with Meridian, like the people's, is sometimes tentative and always respectful of difference and otherness. Like a friend, she follows Meridian, sometimes up close in participation, and at other times from a distance in acts of witness, while Meridian digs out her story in response to her life's slow revolutionary trajectory after the sudden fits and starts of the 1960s. For although revolutions sometimes culminate in explosions, lasting change is prepared for gradually by grubby actions like those Meridian performs in one little

Southern town after another. And true revolutions are never finished; like Meridian's life and story, they illustrate an elliptical pattern of continual change.

—John F. Callahan, *In the African-American Grain: The Pursuit of Voice in Twentieth-Century Black Fiction* (Urbana: University of Illinois Press, 1988): pp. 94–96.

John F. Callahan on the Aura of Voice

[In this extract from his 1988 book *In the African-American Grain: The Pursuit of Voice in Twentieth-Century Black Fiction*, John F. Callahan, the Morgan S. Odell Professor of Humanities at Lewis and Clark College, analyzes Meridian's and Truman's thoughts at the end of Walker's *Meridian*.]

At the end of *Meridian* everything whirls with the motion of change. Meridian and Truman "settle accounts," and at some indeterminate later time Truman declares a brotherly love for his wife, Lynne. "I don't want to do anything but provide for you and be your friend." Perhaps sensing the pain his absence of desire may cause her, he asks a genuine, unrhetorical question: "Can you accept that?" Still Truman pursues the past with Meridian. "I want your love the way I had it a long time ago," he tells her and in his turn accepts painfully her declaration that "my love for you has changed." She has, she claims, set him *free*, and, therefore, she feels free to issue a warning that implies that true friendship between them should influence his inner voice as well as his actions and speech. "You are *not* free, however, to think I am a fool." The remark underscores Meridian's determination to be a serious person in every facet of her experience. Her struggle toward a qualified, continually vulnerable wholeness involves benevolence toward the existence of others, a willingness to see them through their eyes as well as hers. Benevolence now seems Meridian's test for those she is intimate with in her work and her life. For his part, Truman first learns to read Anne-Marion's message to Meridian about the Sojourner tree's newly manifested life. Then, by "the soft wool of her newly grown hair," he understands that Meridian, too, is, in part, "new, sure and ready, even eager, for the world."

As always, Meridian and Truman talk, and at first Truman's spoken words continue to be less genuine than his inner voice. "Your ambivalence," he tells her in a language akin to the *retrick* of the long-head boy in *The Autobiography of Miss Jane Pittman*, "will always be deplored by people who consider themselves revolutionists, and your unorthodox behavior will cause traditionalists to gnash their teeth." Although Truman's feelings have changed, he still speaks words he has been taught to speak and thinks he is supposed to speak. He fails to distinguish his loneliness from Meridian's solitude. For her, true solitude is a sign of potential community; she and those like her "will one day gather at the river. We will watch the evening sun go down. And in the darkness maybe we will know the truth." Her words, the last *spoken* in the novel, are at once prophetic and elemental, metaphysical and sensuous. She includes Truman in her company of solitary silent souls; at least she invites him to join these still marching saints. But she does not stay for an answer because she knows his spoken words lag behind the readiness of his inner voice. Instead, she hugs him freely, naturally—"long, lingeringly (her nose and lips rooting about at his neck, *causing him to laugh*)" (my italics). Then she leaves quickly, in the ascent, the prime of her life—"walking as if hurrying to catch up with someone"— herself maybe and maybe the whole revolving world. She leaves keeping faith with the possibility that she will wear the crazy quilt of her world as Hurston's Janie Crawford draped the net of the horizon around her shoulders.

Lovingly, she leaves Truman in her place to do what is now *their* work. She leaves her sleeping bag behind as a nest to shelter him while his evolving self prepares to act differently toward the world. She knows his loneliness is cause for fear, but she also knows that their conversation has gone as far as it can now. So she leaves him to respond to her inner vision, to that interior dialogue to which she contributes even when not physically present. Her words and parting hug call his inner voice. Free to feel and to cry, Truman takes silent, solitary possession of the gifts she has given him. He identifies the house as his, realizes that the people will come to milk his cow, and that they "would wait patiently for him to *perform*, to take them along the next *guideless* step. Perhaps he would" (my italics). In a spirit of moral contingency and integrity reminiscent of Meridian, Truman senses that among these poor people politics follows from personal worthiness and dignity. He senses, too, that political acts are best performed by a self somehow at once in flux and on the way to completion—a revolutionary self.

Truman's thoughts lead to the resumption of his inner dialogue with Meridian. He *hears* the words of her poem, not as she once wrote them down but as if she were speaking to him now. He feels the room turn with the revolving motion of the world. Like Meridian in her time of dissolution, he yields to a spell of dizziness. As a reflex, he fits his body into Meridian's sleeping bag and puts her cap on his head. Located in her former place, Truman imagines the process of self-discovery and restoration extending to others in his generation. "He had a vision of Anne-Marion herself, arriving, lost, someday, at the door, which would remain open"; he makes no pretense of leading her. Rather, his thoughts return to Meridian, and in careful, disciplined, specific, far-reaching words his newly immediate, complex inner voice communicates the spirit of change for which Meridian and now he, Truman, stand. He "wondered if Meridian knew that the sentence of bearing the conflict in her own soul which she had imposed on herself—and lived through—must now be borne in terror by all the rest of them."

—John F. Callahan, *In the African-American Grain: The Pursuit of Voice in Twentieth-Century Black Fiction* (Urbana: University of Illinois Press, 1988): pp. 128–130.

Plot Summary of
The Color Purple

The ninety-one letters that make up the novel *The Color Purple* span a period of about forty years, from the time of horse and wagon to the automobile. Though the letters are undated, we can establish the time frame through such details as clothing, custom, and speech. Between letters are long lapses that Walker does not fill for us; the reader thereby becomes an obvious collaborator in the making of meaning. Additionally, the protagonist Celie writes in a nonstandard dialect, which Walker has called black folk language. Her letters are characterized by a homely, plainspoken honesty by which Walker, with some success, attempts to reveal Celie's sense of worthlessness and desperation without descending into melodrama.

Celie's **first letter** to God marks the occasion, at age fourteen, of her rape by her father. On this occasion, her mother, sick after childbirth, refuses his advances, and Celie, he says, must "do what ⟨her⟩ mammy wouldn't," but Celie "better not never tell nobody but God. It'd kill your mammy," he tells her. She asks God to send her a sign to explain why these things have happened. At fifteen, Celie is pregnant with her father's child (**letter two**). Her dying mother asks whose baby it is. Celie writes, "I say God's. . . . Finally she ast Where it is? I say God took it." The previous year she had had another baby which, she believes, her father killed. When her mother dies, Celie is left completely unprotected from her father's sexual attacks. But in **letter three** she is relieved and happy, thinking that he has sold the second child, a boy, to "a man an his wife over Monticello." Celie is concerned that her father has turned his sexual attention to her younger sister, Nettie. She vows to protect Nettie, "⟨w⟩ith God help." God seems to have fulfilled Celie's hopes in **letter four**. Her father has remarried and his new wife cares for all his children. Because the couple has sex frequently, Nettie is safe from him.

An older widower, Mr._____, who resembles their father in his brutal ways, now courts Nettie. But Celie accepts this as a natural condition of life. She urges Nettie to keep to her studies and perhaps avoid the fate of their mother, dead of hard work and constant pregnancy. Her father beats Celie for flirting with men in church, an accusation Celie cannot understand (**letter five**). She looks only at women, she writes, "cause I'm not scared of them." Now, she urges Nettie to marry Mr._____, to protect her from their father. Celie writes that she has stopped menstruating, that "she don't bleed no more." Though this would suggest pregnancy, Celie never bears another child. We never learn the reason for her problem.

Shug Avery is introduced in **letter six:** She is Mr._____'s mistress and the reason her father won't allow Nettie to marry Mr._____. Instead, he offers him Celie (**letter seven**). Although, he tells Mr._____, Celie "ain't fresh," having had two children, and is a "bad influence on my other girls," he can do as he likes with her and she won't produce children to burden him. Nettie has replaced Celie as the object of his sexual attentions. Studying a picture of Shug Avery, she imagines that the beautiful woman speaks kindly to her. **Letter eight** reveals the tender relationship between Celie and Nettie. They argue about the world not being round. Mr._____ comes to appraise Celie as if she were a farm animal and agrees to marry her. On her wedding day (**letter nine**), Harpo, the twelve-year-old son of Mr._____, hits her in the head with a rock. She accepts the attack, bandaging her head and resuming her activities as though it were normal. That night, lying beneath Mr._____, she thinks of Nettie and not of her own misery. She imagines herself to be like the beautiful Shug Avery and embraces him. In **letter ten** Celie describes the excitement of a trip into town with her husband. She befriends a woman in a store; the woman holds a baby, Olivia, that Celie intuitively "feels" is her own; she will later learn that this is true. She is told that the baby's father is a reverend. Celie leaves everyone but baby Olivia nameless in her letter to God.

In **letter eleven** Nettie runs away from home to be with Celie. Nettie helps with chores and schooling and teaches Celie to write. Learning is all important to Nettie, and she urges Celie to fight back. Nettie leaves, promising to write, but Celie ends the letter by saying that she never did. (Nettie does write, but Celie will not receive the letters for many years. When she does, they will form the structure for the rest of the novel.) A comic interlude in **letter twelve** gives Celie more information about the fascinating Shug. Mr._____'s two sisters, Kate and Carrie, come to inspect the new bride and gossip about everyone, including Mr._____'s first wife. They approve of Celie's housekeeping, cooking, and stepmothering skills. As for Shug, however, they both think she's "too black," a prejudice Celie had not thought about and which she rejects. Kate tells Celie that she deserves "more than this." This idea is central to the novel as it shapes Celie's emotional development.

Five years pass before Celie writes another letter (**letter thirteen**). Harpo, her wedding-day assailant, is seventeen; Celie is about twenty-five. Her husband has savagely beaten her, and she tells God her survival technique: "I make myself wood. . . . Celie, you a tree." Harpo, a gentle, if immature boy, wants to marry. In **letter fourteen** Celie eagerly awaits the arrival of Shug Avery, and in **letter fifteen** she reveals that, as long as she can share her husband with so fantastic and beautiful a woman as Shug, Celie will be happy.

Letters sixteen and **seventeen** focus upon Harpo, "strong in body but weak in will," and his desire to marry Sofia Butler, whose "daddy say Harpo not good enough for her." Harpo's mother had been shot by her boyfriend and died in Harpo's arms. He talks this over with Celie and decides that "if [Sofia] be big I got a right to be with her, good enough or no." Harpo brings Sofia home (**letter eighteen**) but, though he loves Sofia, he is frustrated that he can't "make her mind." "Beat her," Celie advises (**letter nineteen**). When Sofia confronts her about this and demands to know why she would tell Harpo to beat her (**letter twenty**), Celie admits "I say it cause I'm jealous of you. . . . cause you do what I can't." Sofia, unlike Celie, fights Harpo's control over her. The women become close after this.

Mr._____ brings Shug Avery, the "Queen Honeybee," home to recuperate from some unspecified illness (**letter twenty-two**). Celie observes that Shug is indeed ill, but that "she more evil than my mama and that keep her alive (**letter twenty-three**)." From Shug she learns that her husband's name is Albert. She bathes Shug (**letter twenty-four**) and is startled by her own feelings: "First time I got the full sight of Shug Avery long black body with it black plum nipples, look like her mouth, I thought I had turned into a man." Celie spends as much time as she can with Shug, coaxing her to eat (**letter twenty-five**), combing her hair, and, finally, Celie's sensuous attentions relax her (**letter twenty-six**) and they become friends. Both Celie and Albert are in love with Shug Avery.

Sofia is puzzled about Harpo's odd behavior (**letter twenty-eight**): He has been eating everything in sight and is starting to gain noticeable weight. Celie discovers, as does Harpo, in conversation with him the next night, that, since he cannot control Sofia as his father controls Celie, he will try to equal her in bulk. He vomits and that ends that problem. But Sofia is tired of Harpo's immaturity and she goes, with the children, to stay with her sister (**letters thirty** and **thirty-one**). Harpo turns their house into a juke joint (**letters thirty-two** and **thirty-three**) where Shug Avery agrees to sing, drawing a profitable crowd (**letters thirty-four** to **thirty-six**). Celie and Albert go together to Harpo's: "He love looking at Shug. I love looking at Shug." Celie's "heart hurt⟨s⟩" because Shug looks only at Albert. But Shug sings what she calls "Miss Celie's song. . . . Cause she scratched it out of my head when I was sick." This gift from Shug to Celie is evidence of the spiritual bond between them. Shug instructs Celie in techniques of masturbation in **letter thirty-five** and informs Celie that, since she has never experienced sexual pleasure, she is "still a virgin."

Letters thirty-seven through **forty-four** focus upon the brutal—white—social retribution against Sofia for her independence of spirit. After she curtly dismisses the mayor's wife's offer of a job as maid to her ("Hell, no," she said) the mayor slaps her. Sofia responds in kind and is beaten almost to death by the police and sent to prison. Years later she is released on probation to work as maid in the mayor's house where she lives as a virtual slave, allowed to see her children only once a year. "White folks is a miracle of affliction, say Sofia."

In **letters forty-five** and **forty-eight** Celie writes about the increasing closeness of her relationship with Shug. In **letters forty-nine** through **fifty-one** Shug works to find the letters she and Celie are sure that Nettie has written—and that Albert has kept from her all these years. In letter **forty-nine** Shug gives Celie the letter from Nettie hidden in Mr._____'s coat pocket. They find all Nettie's letters hidden in a trunk in **letter fifty-one**.

Nettie's first letters to Celie (**letters fifty-two** to **fifty-eight**) reveal that Celie's children were adopted by the missionary couple who had taken her in. Nettie has gone to Africa with them. "It is a miracle, isn't it?" Nettie writes, "And no doubt impossible for you to believe." In **letters fifty-nine** to **sixty-one** Celie writes briefly to God to report that Shug has kept her from killing Mr._____. Knowing Nettie is still alive makes her "strut a little bit." But the children worry her: "Incest part of the devil's plan." Nettie writes about

Olinka, the African village, in **letters sixty-two** to **sixty-seven**. She writes about the racism among blacks and whites and the different ways in which it is imagined and configured. What rise above racism, sexual love, and children are the friendships and understandings between women, something Nettie writes to Celie about, and something Celie has learned as well. She also writes about the destruction of Olinka by the European planters and roadbuilders.

In **letters sixty-eight** and **sixty-nine** Celie learns that her children are not, after all, products of actual incest because Fonso is not her real father. She writes that the colors of wildflowers and images of spring are everywhere, even to the "folkspants" that Celie has made for herself and Shug. Letter sixty-nine is the first that Celie addresses directly to Nettie. In **letters seventy-one** and **seventy-two** Nettie writes that Corrine, the missionary wife, is near death and refuses to believe that Olivia and Adam are really Celie's children and not Nettie's. Quilts have appeared throughout the text, either as work or as comforting gifts, and here Nettie searches to find one that will remind Corrine of her long-ago encounter with Celie when Olivia was a baby. This way, Nettie knows, Corrine will not die unhappy. After Corrine's death, Nettie and Samuel, Corrine's husband, marry.

Celie has a crisis of faith in **letters seventy-four** to **eighty**. She resents the pain and injustices of the past. Shug persuasively argues with her about God, concluding, "I think it pisses God off if you walk by the color purple in a field somewhere and don't notice it." Celie admits, "Now that my eyes opening, I feels like a fool. . . . You have to git man off your eyeball, before you can see anything a'tall." Celie's pants-making business is a success. Harpo has become like a father to his own father, Albert, bathing him, caring for him, holding him while he sleeps. He has made his father give Celie the rest of Nettie's letters. Nettie writes to Celie (**letters eighty-one** and **eighty-two**) that she and Samuel were married on a trip to England to seek funds for Olinka from the churches and the Missionary Society. She tells of Corrine's Aunt Theodosia who received a medal from the King of Belgium for her relief work. She is taken to task, however, by W. E. B. Du Bois (here "Du Boyce") who tells her that she should regard it instead as a "symbol of her unwitting complicity . . . in the exterminat(ion of) thousands and thousands of African peoples." Nettie writes of Celie's son, Adam, "Did I tell you he writes verses? And loves to sing? He's a son to make you proud." Of her own tie to

Celie she confides, "⟨A⟩ll things look brighter because I have a loving soul to share them with."

In **letter eighty-three** Celie writes to Nettie that Fonso, their "Pa," has died and that the house is theirs, "A house big enough for us and our children, for your husband and Shug. Now you can come home because you have a home to come to." But Celie receives a telegram from the Department of Defense (**letter eighty-six**) telling her that Nettie, Samuel, and her children are dead; the ship that carried them were sunk by German mines located off Gibraltar. Celie also writes, "all the letters I wrote to you over the years come back unopen."

But Nettie is not dead. In **letter eighty-seven** she writes to Celie of her new understanding of God, one not unlike Celie's: "Most people think ⟨God⟩ has to look like something or someone . . . but we don't. And not being tied to what God looks like, frees us." Thirty years have passed since Nettie left Celie at Mr._____'s house. In **letters eighty-eight** to **ninety** all conflicts seem to be resolved save the puzzle of racism, and the extended family is reunited: "And us so happy. Matter of fact, I think this the youngest us ever felt." ❋

List of Characters in
The Color Purple

Celie is a nearly illiterate, 14-year-old black girl living in Georgia. Believing she was raped and impregnated by her father and that he murdered at least one of their children, she writes letters to God. Through these letters she speaks, matter-of-factly, about this terrible knowledge; God, she feels, is someone who loves her and is the only person she can talk to. She wonders why all this has happened to her and feels to be of such little worth that she will not even sign her name to these letters. She marries a cruel man who had wanted to marry her sister, Nettie; surprisingly, the arrival of her husband's mistress in the house to recuperate is the start of Celie's journey to independence. In the course of the novel, her close friendships with Shug, Nettie, and Sofia help her to mature into a confident woman.

Lilly "Shug" Avery is a flashy jazz singer and Albert's mistress. Her nickname, "Shug," which she chose for herself, suggests a sweetness directly opposed to the uncompromising honesty, self-centeredness, and manipulative power that constitute her nature. Although she is the mother of three of Albert's children, he refuses to marry her after the death of his first wife and instead marries Celie. But Shug is an original, a black woman as improvisational and innovative in her approach to living as jazz itself. She helps Celie to discover love, a new self-esteem, and a wholly original relationship with whatever God is.

Albert _____ is Celie's husband. Both evil and weak, Albert brutally mistreats Celie, but his affection for Shug reveals him to be human. His weakness is rooted in his lack of self-knowledge and his subservience to his own father, whose attitudes he emulates. He never asks Shug to marry him, although he never hides his love for her, because he is afraid of her strength, her control over him. He had wanted to marry Nettie, but had to settle for the "spoiled" daughter, Celie. When both Celie and Shug abandon him, his character is gradually transformed; he realizes that, by his cruelty to Celie, he deprived himself of a good woman.

Sofia is Celie's daughter-in-law. Much younger than Celie, she is a new kind of southern black woman, one who demands equality in her marriage to Harpo. She is a generous sister and friend, and a devoted mother. After a public altercation with the white mayor and his wife, Sofia goes to prison where she is severely beaten, and her strength to resist the barriers to her independent spirit is almost crushed.

Nettie is Celie's sister and the girl Celie's husband Albert had wanted to marry. She travels with a missionary couple and, unwittingly, Celie's children, to Africa where she finds purpose and love. After the death of the reverend's wife, she and the reverend marry and she returns to Celie with the grown children.

Harpo is Albert's son and Sofia's husband. Although immature and often a disappointment to his strong and energetic wife, his love for Sofia endures despite their separation and her imprisonment.

Fonso is Celie's and Nettie's stepfather—and father of Olivia and Adam.

Olivia and **Adam** are Celie's son and daughter, reared in Africa by missionaries who adopted them at birth. ❀

Critical Views on
The Color Purple

GLORIA STEINEM ON STORYTELLING STYLE

[Gloria Steinem is a writer, journalist, feminist leader, and political activist. She was a co-founder of *Ms.* magazine and is author of *Outrageous Acts and Everyday Rebellions* (1983) and *Revolution from Within: A Book of Self-Esteem* (1992). In this essay, she praises the storytelling style of Celie in *The Color Purple*.]

The storytelling style of *The Color Purple* makes it irresistible to read. The words belong to Celie, the downest and outest of women. Because she must survive against impossible odds, because she has no one to talk to, she writes about her life in the guise of letters to God. When she discovers her much-loved lost sister is not dead after all but is living in Africa, she writes letters to Nettie instead. The point is, she must tell someone the truth and confirm her existence. ⟨. . .⟩

The result is an inviting, dead-honest, surprising novel that is the successful culmination of Alice Walker's longer and longer trips outside the safety of Standard English narration, and into the words of her characters. Here, she takes the leap completely. There is no third person to distance the reader from events. We are inside Celie's head.

And Celie turns out to be a no-nonsense, heartrending story-teller with a gift for cramming complicated turns of events and whole life histories into very few words. Like E. L. Doctorow in *Ragtime*, the rhythm of the telling adds to the momentum of suspense—but what he did with an episodic style and pace of chapters, Celie can do with the placement of a line, a phrase, a verb. ⟨. . .⟩

Reviewers should also understand why Alice Walker has always preferred to describe her characters' speech as "black folk English," not "dialect"; a word she feels has been used in a condescending, racist way. When these people talk, there are no self-conscious apostrophes and contradictions to assure us that the writer, of course, really knows what the proper spelling and grammar should be. There are no quotation marks to keep us at our distance. Celie just writes her heart out, putting words down the way they feel and sound. Pretty soon you can't imagine why anyone would bother to write any other way.

The second pleasure of *The Color Purple* is watching people redeem themselves and grow, or wither and turn inward, according to the ways they do or don't work out the moral themes in their lives. In the hands of this author, morality is not an external dictate. It doesn't matter if you love the wrong people, or have children with more than one of them, or whether you have money, go to church, or obey the laws. What matters is cruelty, violence, keeping the truth from others who need it, suppressing someone's will or talent, taking more than you need from people or nature, and failing to choose for yourself. It's the internal morality of dignity, autonomy, and balance.

What also matters is the knowledge that everybody, no matter how poor or passive on the outside, has these possibilities inside.

By the end of the novel, we believe that this poor, nameless patch of land in the American South is really the world—and vice versa. Conversations between Celie and Shug have brought us theories of philosophy, ethics, and metaphysics; all with a world vision that seems more complete for proceeding from the bottom up. The color purple, an odd miracle of nature, symbolizes the miracle of human possibilities.

—Gloria Steinem, "Do You Know This Woman? She Knows You: A Profile of Alice Walker," *Ms.* 10, no. 12 (June 1982): pp. 35–37, 89–94.

PETER S. PRESCOTT ON REDEMPTIVE LOVE

[Peter S. Prescott is an author and critic. He is editor of *The Norton Book of American Short Stories* (1988), and author of *Never in Doubt: Critical Essays on American Books (1972–1985)* (1986), *The Child Savers: Juvenile Justice Observed* (1981), and *A Darkening Green: Notes from the Silent Generation* (1974). Here, he explains that female bonding is required for the redemptive love necessary for survival.]

Because I have an eerie feeling that any attempt I make to describe what happens in this story is likely to start the summer rush for the beaches, I want to say at once that The *Color Purple* is an American novel of permanent importance, that rare sort of book which (in Norman Mailer's felicitous phrase) amounts to "a diversion in the fields of dread." Alice Walker excels at making difficulties for herself and then transcending them. To cite an example: her story begins at about the point that most Greek tragedies reserve for the climax, then becomes by immeasurably small steps a comedy which works its way toward acceptance, serenity and joy. To cite another: her narrative advances entirely by means of letters that are either never delivered or are delivered too late for a response, and most of these are written in a black English that Walker appears to have modified artfully for general consumption.

The letters begin with Celie addressing herself to God because she's ashamed to tell anyone else. Celie is black, ugly, not good at school work; she lives in rural Georgia in this century's second decade and is 14 when the man she takes to be her father begins to rape her. She bears this man two children, who are taken away; at his insistence, she marries a man who would rather have had her younger sister, Nettie. Others call Celie's husband Albert, but she cannot; unable to muster his name in her letters, she calls him "Mr.____." "You black, you pore, you ugly," Albert tells his wife, "you a woman . . . you nothing at all." Albert invites to their home his old mistress, a blues singer named Shug Avery, who arrives ill, with "the nasty woman disease." This event, which should break up any household, proves oddly restorative; a bond between Celie and Shug develops, almost to the exclusion of the useless Albert.

In time—the course of this novel covers more than 30 years—Celie discovers that the despicable Albert has been withholding letters written to her by Nettie, who has gone to West Africa as an apprentice missionary with the couple who adopted Celie's children. . . . Celie now writes to Nettie letters that her sister never receives. There is, in this parallel correspondence in which no letter ever hopes for an answer, something deeply moving: these sisters need each other desperately, but each must mature and survive without response from the other.

Love redeems, meanness kills—that is *The Color Purple*'s principal theme, the theme of most of the world's great fiction. Nevertheless—

and this is why this black woman's novel will survive a white man's embrace—the redemptive love that is celebrated here is selective, even prickly. White folk figure rarely in its pages and never to their advantage, and black men are recovered only to the extent that they buckle down to housework and let women attend to business. For Walker, redemptive love requires female bonding. The bond liberates women from men, who are predators at worst, idle at best.

In the traditional manner, Walker ends her comedy with a dance, or more precisely with a barbecue. "White people busy celebrating they independence from England July 4th," says Celie's stepson, "so most black folk don't have to work. Us can spend the day celebrating each other." In this novel, the celebration has been painfully earned.

—Peter S. Prescott, "A Long Road to Liberation," *Newsweek* (21 June 1982): pp. 67–68.

MEL WATKINS ON FOLK VOICE

[Mel Watkins has taught economics at the University of Toronto for more than forty years. He is a social critic, political activist, writer, editor, and author. His books include *On the Real Side* (1994) and *Report of the Task Force on the Structure of Canadian Industry* (*The Watkins Report*). In this essay, he argues that the folk voice of the novel makes it convincing.]

Without doubt, Alice Walker's latest novel is her most impressive. No mean accomplishment, since her previous books . . . have elicited almost unanimous praise for Miss Walker as a lavishly gifted writer. *The Color Purple,* while easily satisfying that claim, brings into sharper focus many of the diverse themes that threaded their way through her past work.⟨ . . .⟩

Most prominent ⟨of the book's major themes⟩ is the estrangement and violence that mark the relationships between Miss Walker's black men and women. ⟨. . .⟩

⟨Miss Walker has⟩ dealt with ⟨this⟩ subject before. In her collection *You Can't Keep a Good Woman Down*, two stories ("Porn" and "Coming Apart") assess the sexual disaffection among black couples. And the saintly heroine of the novel *Meridian* is deserted by a black lover who then marries a white civil-rights worker, whom he also later abandons. In *Meridian*, however, the friction between black men and women is merely one of several themes; in *The Color Purple* the role of male domination in the frustration of black women's struggle for independence is clearly the focus.

Miss Walker explores the estrangement of her men and women through a triangular love affair. It is Shug Avery who forces Albert to stop brutalizing Celie, and it is Shug with whom Celie first consummates a satisfying and reciprocally loving relationship. ⟨. . .⟩

What makes Miss Walker's exploration so indelibly affecting is the choice of a narrative style that, without the intrusion of the author, forces intimate identification with ⟨Celie⟩. . . . Most of the letters that comprise this epistolary novel are written by Celie, although correspondence from Nettie is included in the latter part of the book. Initially, some readers may be put off by Celie's knothole view of the world, particularly since her letters are written in dialect and from the perspective of a naïve, uneducated adolescent. ⟨. . .⟩

As the novel progresses, however, and as Celie grows in experience, her observations become sharper and more informed; the letters take on authority and the dialect, once accepted, assumes a lyrical cadence of its own. ⟨. . .⟩

The cumulative effect is a novel that is convincing because of the authenticity of its folk voice. And refreshingly, it is not just the two narrator-correspondents who come vividly alive in this tale. A number of memorable female characters emerge. There is Shug Avery, whose pride, independence and appetite for living act as a catalyst for Celie and others, and Sophia, whose rebellious spirit leads her not only to desert her overbearing husband but also to challenge the social order of the racist community in which she lives.

If there is a weakness in this novel—besides the somewhat pallid portraits of the males—it is Nettie's correspondence from Africa. While Nettie's letters broaden and reinforce the theme of female oppression by describing customs of the Olinka tribe that parallel some found in the American South, they are often mere monologues on African history. Appearing, as they do, after Celie's intensely subjective voice has been established, they seem lackluster and intrusive.

These are only quibbles, however, about a striking and consummately well-written novel. Alice Walker's choice and effective handling of the epistolary style has enabled her to tell a poignant tale of women's struggle for equality and independence without either the emotional excess of her previous novel *Meridian* or the polemical excess of her short-story collection *You Can't Keep a Good Woman Down.*

—Mel Watkins, "Some Letters Went to God," *The New York Times Book Review* (25 July 1982): p. 7.

ROBERT TOWERS ON THE RHYTHMS OF DIALECT

[Robert Towers (1923–1995) was a novelist, critic, and professor of writing at Columbia University. He published numerous essays on contemporary American and British fiction, as well as novels, including *The Summoning* (1983), *The Monkey Watcher* (1964), and *The Necklace of Kali* (1960). Here, he discusses Walker's writing skills as reflected in *The Color Purple.*]

There is nothing cool or throwaway in Alice Walker's attitude toward the materials of her fiction. The first book by this exceptionally productive novelist, poet, and short-story writer to come to my notice was *Meridian* (1976), an impassioned account of the spiritual progress of a young black woman, Meridian Hill, during the civil-rights struggle of the 1960s and its aftermath. . . . Though beset by serious structural problems and other lapses of craft, *Meridian* remains the most impressive fictional treatment of the "Movement" that I have yet read.

In *The Color Purple* Alice Walker moves backward in time, setting her story roughly (the chronology is kept vague) between 1916 and 1942—a period during which the post-Reconstruction settlement of black status remained almost unaltered in the Deep South. Drawing upon what must be maternal and grandmaternal accounts as well as upon her own memory and observation, Miss Walker, who is herself under forty, exposes us to a way of life that for the most part existed beyond or below the reach of fiction and that has hitherto been made available to us chiefly through tape-recorded reminiscences: the life of the poor, rural Southern blacks as it was experienced by their womenfolk.

I cannot gauge the general accuracy of Miss Walker's account ⟨of Celie's life⟩ or the degree to which it may be colored by current male-female antagonisms within the black community. ⟨. . .⟩ I did note certain improbabilities: it seems unlikely that a woman of Celie's education would have applied the word "amazons" to a group of feisty sisters or that Celie, in the 1930s, would have found fulfillment in designing and making pants for women. In any case, *The Color Purple* has more serious faults than its possible feminist bias. Alice Walker still has a lot to learn about plotting and structuring what is clearly intended to be a realistic novel. The revelations involving the fate of Celie's lost babies and the identity of her real father seem crudely contrived—the stuff of melodrama or fairy tales.

The extended account of Nettie's experience in Africa, to which she has gone with a black missionary couple and their two adopted children, is meant to be a counterweight to Celie's story but it lacks authenticity—not because Miss Walker is ignorant of Africa ⟨. . .⟩ but because she has failed to endow Nettie with her own distinctive voice; the fact that Nettie is better educated than Celie—and a great reader—should not have drained her epistolary style of all personal flavor, leaving her essentially uncharacterized, a mere reporter of events. The failure to find an interesting idiom for a major figure like Nettie is especially damaging in an epistolary novel, which is at best a difficult genre for a twentieth-century writer, posing its own special problems of momentum and credibility.

Fortunately, inadequacies which might tell heavily against another novel seem relatively insignificant in view of the one great challenge which Alice Walker has triumphantly met: the conversion, in Celie's letters, of a subliterate dialect into a medium of remarkable expressiveness, color, and poignancy. I find it impossible to imagine Celie apart from her language; through it, not only a memorable and infinitely touching character but a whole submerged world is vividly called into being. Miss Walker knows how to avoid the excesses of literal transcription while remaining faithful to the spirit and rhythms of Black English. I can think of no other novelist who has so successfully tapped the poetic resources of the idiom.

—Robert Towers, "Good Men Are Hard to Find," *The New York Times Review of Books* (12 August 1982): pp. 35–36.

DINITIA SMITH ON THE SOUTHERN FICTIONAL TRADITION

[Dinitia Smith is a novelist, critic, and journalist. Her articles appear in the *New York Times*, and she is author of *The Illusionist* (1997) and *Remember This* (1989). In this essay, Smith discusses the southern fiction tradition and how it is evident in the novels of Alice Walker, particularly *The Color Purple*.]

As admirers of *The Third Life of Grange Copeland* and *Meridian* already know, to read an Alice Walker novel is to enter the country of surprise. It is to be admitted to the world of rural black women, a world long neglected by most whites, perhaps out of ignorance, perhaps out of willed indifference. The loss is ours, for the lives of these women are so extraordinary in their tragedy, their culture, their humor and their courage that we are immediately gripped by them.

No writer has made the intimate hurt of racism more palpable than Walker. In one of ⟨*The Color Purple*'s⟩ most rending scenes, Celie's stepdaughter-in-law, Sophia, is sentenced to work as a maid in the white mayor's house for "sassing" the mayor's wife. In a fit of magnanimity, the mayor's wife offers to drive Sophia home to see her children, whom she hasn't laid eyes on in five years. The reunion lasts only fifteen minutes—then the mayor's wife insists that Sophia drive her home.

The Color Purple is about the struggle between redemption and revenge. And the chief agency of redemption, Walker is saying, is the strength of the relationships between women: their friendships, their love, their shared oppression. Even the white mayor's family is redeemed when his daughter cares for Sophia's sick daughter.

There is a note of tendentiousness here, though. The men in this book change *only* when their women join together and rebel—and then, the change is so complete as to be unrealistic. It was hard for me to believe that a person as violent, brooding and just plain nasty as Mr.—— could ever become that sweet, quiet man smoking and chatting on the porch.

Walker's didacticism is especially evident in Nettie's letters from Africa, which make up a large portion of the book.

Walker's politics are not the problem—*of course* sexism and racism are terrible, *of course* women should band together to help each other. But the politics have to be incarnated in complex, contradictory characters—characters to whom the novelist grants the freedom to act, as it were, on their own.

I wish Walker had let herself be carried along more by her language, with all its vivid figures of speech, Biblical cadences, distinctive grammar and true-to-life starts and stops. The pithy, direct black folk idiom of *The Color Purple* is in the end its greatest strength, reminding us that if Walker is sometimes an ideologue, she is also a poet.

Despite its occasional preachiness, *The Color Purple* marks a major advance for Walker's art. At its best, and at least half the book is superb, it places her in the company of Faulkner, from whom she appears to have learned a great deal: the use of a shifting first-person narrator, for instance, and the presentation of a complex story from a naïve point of view, like that of 14-year-old Celie. Walker has not turned her back on the Southern fictional tradition. She has absorbed it and made it her own. By infusing the black experience into the Southern novel, she enriches both it and us.

—Dinitia Smith, "'Celie, You a Tree'," *The Nation* (4 September 1982): pp. 181–183.

[Elizabeth Bartelme is Star Adjunct Professor of English at Hofstra University. She has edited fifteen books by Daniel Berrigan and is co-editor of *Franklin D. Roosevelt: The Man, the Myth, the Era* (1987). Bartelme discusses how the characters in the novel learn to accept whatever life throws at them.]

In this arresting and touching novel ⟨*The Color Purple*⟩, Alice Walker creates a woman so believable, so lovable, that Celie, the downtrodden, semi-literate, rural black woman joins a select company of fictional women whom it is impossible to forget.

Alice Walker is, of course, a feminist and she understands well the circumstances that force a woman into an anti-man stance. Her gallery of women are living examples of man's inhumanity to women: Sophia, wife of Harpo, Albert's eldest son, who only wanting to be herself and not the fantasy woman Harpo thinks she ought to be, changes from a warm, happy woman to a bitter paranoic who only wants to get through her life without killing anyone. Mary Alice, "Squeak," who takes Sophia's place with Harpo when the latter is jailed for sassing the mayor's wife (white), and who allows her uncle, the warden to rape her in exchange for Sophia's freedom. Even Shug, the indomitable, has her share of suffering at men's hands. Only Nettie ⟨. . .⟩ seems to have escaped the general mayhem, and she is a curiously colorless character. Her letters, by comparison with Celie's are pedantic, her nature prim. The other women leap out of the book, Nettie stays safely within its confines, as does her husband, Samuel.

But Alice Walker is too much of an artist to write a purely political novel, and so her feminist impulse does not prevent her from allowing her characters, women and men, to grow and change. The men in her story lead miserable lives, too, but like their women they begin to come to terms with what life doles out to them, and accept it. And the women turn from rage to acceptance as well. One of the best scenes in the book occurs as Mr.____ and Celie sit sewing on the front porch, old now and calm together, and talking about the lessons life has taught them. Albert tells her he has learned to wonder, to wonder about all the things that happen and "the more I wonder, he say, the more I love.

"And people start to love you back, I bet, I say.
"They do, he say, surprise. Harpo seem to love me. Sophia and the children . . . "
They go on sewing and talking and waiting for Shug to come home, and Celie says to herself, "If she come, I be happy. If she don't, I be content.
"And then I figure this the lesson I was supposed to learn."

And so bitterness leaches out into a hard-won wisdom, and the lively characters of Alice Walker's invention become human beings with a life of their own. She is a remarkable novelist, sometimes compared to Toni Morrison, but with a strong, individual voice and vision of her own, and a delicious humor that pervades the book and tempers the harshness of the lives of its people.

Opening with a dedication to the Spirit, the novel ends with a postscript: "I thank everybody in this book for coming. A. W., author and medium." This reader's thanks to the medium; may she call up hosts in the future.

—Elizabeth Bartelme, "Victory Over Bitterness," *Commonweal* 110, no. 3 (11 February 1983): pp. 93–94.

TRUDIER HARRIS ON THE MYTH OF THE AMERICAN DREAM

[Trudier Harris is J. Carlyle Sitterson Professor of English at the University of North Carolina at Chapel Hill. Her works include *The Power of the Porch: The Storyteller's Craft in Zora Neale Hurston, Gloria Naylor, and Randall Kenan* (1997), *Black Women in the Fiction of James Baldwin* (1985), and *Exorcising Blackness* (1984) and she is co-editor of *The Oxford Companion to African American Literature* (1997). In this essay Harris discusses how Walker sees the American Dream as, essentially, a myth, especially for black Americans.]

From the beginning of the novel, even as Walker presents Celie's sexual abuse by her stepfather, there is an element of fantasy in the book. Celie becomes the ugly duckling who will eventually be redeemed through suffering. This trait links her to all the heroines of fairy tales from Cinderella to Snow White. Instead of the abusive stepmother as the villain, the stepfather plays that role. He devalues Celie in direct proportion to Nettie's valuing of her; unfortunately, as an inexperienced rather than an adult godmother, Nettie lacks the ability to protect Celie. The clash between youth and age, between power and powerlessness begins the mixed-media approach of the novel. Celie's predicament may be real, but she is forced to deal with it in terms that are antithetical to the reality of her condition.

The fabulist/fairy-tale mold of the novel is ultimately incongruous with and does not serve well to frame its message. When things turn out happily in those traditional tales, we are asked to affirm the basic pattern and message: Good triumphs over evil. But what does *The Color Purple* affirm? What were all those women who applauded approving of? It affirms, first of all, patience and long-suffering— perhaps to a greater degree than that exhibited by Cinderella or by the likes of Elizabeth Grimes in James Baldwin's *Go Tell It on the Mountain*. In true fairy-tale fashion, it affirms passivity; heroines in those tales do little to help themselves. It affirms silence in the face of, if not actual allegiance to, cruelty. It affirms secrecy concerning violence and violation. It affirms, saddest of all, the myth of the American Dream becoming a reality for black Americans, even those who are "dirt poor," as one of my colleagues phrased it, and those who are the "downest" and "outest." The fable structure thereby perpetuates a lie in holding out to blacks a non-existent or minimally existent hope for a piece of that great American pie. The clash of characters who presumably contend with and in the real world with the idealistic, suprarealistic quality and expectations of fairy-tale worlds places a burden on the novel that diffuses its message and guarantees possibilities for unintended interpretations.

With its mixture of message, form, and character, *The Color Purple* reads like a political shopping list of all the IOUs Walker felt that it was time to repay. She pays homage to the feminists by portraying a woman who struggles through adversity to assert herself against almost impossible odds. She pays homage to the lesbians by portraying a relationship between two women that reads like a schoolgirl fairy tale in its ultimate adherence to the convention of the happy resolution. She pays homage to black nationalists by opposing colonialism, and to Pan Africanism by suggesting that yes, indeed, a black American does understand and sympathize with the plight of her black brothers and sisters thousands of miles across the ocean. And she adds in a few other obeisances—to career-minded women in the characters of Mary Agnes and Shug, to born-again male feminists in the character of Albert, and to black culture generally in the use of the blues and the folk idiom.

I *will* teach *The Color Purple* again—precisely because of the teachability engendered by its controversiality. I will be angry again because I am not a spectator to what happens to Celie; for me, the novel *demands* participation. I will continue to react to all praise of the novel by asserting that mere praise ignores the responsibility that goes along with it—we must clarify as much as we can the reasons that things are being praised and enumerate as best we can the consequences of that praise. I will continue to read and re-read the novel, almost in self-defense against the continuing demands for discussions and oral evaluations of it. Perhaps—and other black women may share this response—I am caught in a love/hate relationship with *The Color Purple*; though my crying out against it might be comparable to spitting into a whirlwind in an effort to change its course, I shall nevertheless purse my lips.

—Trudier Harris, "On *The Color Purple*, Stereotypes and Silence," *Black American Literature Forum* 18, no. 4 (Winter 1984): pp. 155–161.

BETTYE J. PARKER-SMITH ON SOVEREIGN WOMEN

[Bettye J. Parker-Smith's essay "Alice Walker's Women: In Search of Some Peace of Mind" originally appeared in *Black Women Writers (1950–1980): A Critical Evaluation* (1984). In this excerpt from that article, Parker-Smith discusses the women of *The Color Purple*.]

⟨*The Color Purple*⟩ shows Alice Walker's growth as a writer. And, in this masterpiece that exceeds its limits as a work of fiction, she elevates Black women to the height of sovereignty. They wear the royal robe of purple. In her early works, women used their fragile strength to love everybody and anybody except themselves. Now, robed in purple, they receive and accept the *right* to love themselves and each other. Love of self energizes them to the point that they break their chains of enslavement, change their own worlds, time and Black men. They are prepared to fight—eye for an eye, tooth for a tooth. And they remain women—cry when they need to, laugh when they want to, straighten their hair if they take a notion. They change their economic, political, and moral status, with love.

⟨The⟩ women in *Purple* build a wall of camaraderie around themselves. They share in each other's pain, sorrow, laughter, and dreams. They applaud each other's achievements. And they come to each other's rescue. They are sisters in body as well as in spirit and the spirit *cannot* be broken. They found God in themselves and "they loved *her* fiercely."

⟨To⟩ transmute any part of the Holy Trinity to female would suggest to these women a lesbian notion, which is not only immoral and unnatural but sacrilegious as well. Walker's women, traditional then, who found solace in the church, accepted the church in the ways that they could best relate to it, time and circumstances playing important roles. Her modern women find that God is within.

Purple opens with a warning: "You better not never tell nobody but God. It'd kill your mammy." This statement introduces a long list of pain-stricken letters to God. Bosom buddy though God may be, she must use her all-knowing power to recognize the writers of these letters because they bear no signatures. For the character writer, Celie, being omnipotent is quite enough. What she needs is to share her burdens, be taken off the cross, and find a way to save herself. She does find a way and it works because, as she discovers, God *is* herself.

The women in Alice Walker's fiction ⟨. . .⟩ are a disturbing bunch indeed. For the most part, they do not understand the complexity of their problem, and because their limited worlds cannot assist them they are destined to operate haphazardly. They vacillate between the bottle and the Bible and spend a lot of time on their knees. The distinctive feature of these women is the tremendous quality with which they carry their suffering. Some are generous and proud. Some are forgiving even to the men who mistreat them. Some are trusting and patient. The new women overcome insurmountable odds to change their condition. They are all resilient to a point. All of these qualities contribute to the success of Walker's literary style and effect.

In forcing her readers to face the truth, she carries them beyond the normality or abnormality of an experience. In blowing the breath of life into her characters, she carries the reader to the edge of the cliff—to the point where the balloon is ready to burst. She operates the way of a good gumbo maker; the roux must remain on the fire until the point of burning. It takes skill and know-how to be able to recognize that point. She uses imagery, often intangible, grass-roots form, to connect her characters to the South: flowers, quilts, cotton stalks, wasps' nests. Plant life (often in the form of petunias) is a consistent image in her fiction as well as her poetry. Her sense of humor allows the reader to move through her fiction without becoming overburdened by its pain. Plants, often present in her death scenes or at the end of some tragic moment, have a germinating quality. They symbolize hope. As a major modern writer, Alice Walker continues to water her purple petunias. The height that she can climb as an American literary contributor cannot even be suggested. What is evident, however, is that her women are now finding some peace of mind.

—Bettye J. Parker-Smith, "Alice Walker's Women: In Search of Some Peace of Mind" in *Black Women Writers (1950–1980): A Critical Evaluation*, ed. Mari Evans (Garden City, N.Y.: Doubleday/Anchor, 1984): pp. 478–493.

GEORGE STADE ON WOMEN AND MEN

[George Stade is professor of English at Columbia University. He has published hundreds of critical reviews and articles and has been editor-in-chief of *Columbia Essays* on *Modern Writers*. His novel, *Confessions of a Lady-Killer*, was published in 1979. In his essay, Stade finds in *The Color Purple* a view that "masculinity is radical evil . . . the causeless cause of all that's wrong with the world."]

The Color Purple has its deepest tinges of women's liberation at its conclusion, with the establishment of a utopian commune presided over by the heroine and her female lover, although a couple of womanish men are allowed to hang around, so long as they behave themselves. But the novel is not feminist—it does not argue the equality of the sexes; it dramatizes, rather, the virtues of women and the vices of men.

⟨With⟩ a few telling exceptions ⟨the men⟩ are brutal in the flesh because they are impoverished of spirit. They are pitiless when they are not self-pitying. They are misogynist and they are pedophobic ("he hate children and he hate where they come from"). They are petty, spiteful, "hurtful," and treacherous. They are also arrogant, complacent, lazy, insensitive, incompetent, vain, inartistic, contemptuous of women, but quick to take credit for their work. Above all, they are lechers, mechanical monsters of sexual appetite.

What makes men so awful we never learn. The male characters in this novel, all black, are not, as we might think, made awful by their mistreatment at the hands of whites. Nettie's letters from Africa, where the men are just as awful, make precisely that point. ("Wherever there's a man, there's trouble.") We do learn that Harpo, against the grain, is awful to women because that is what his father, Mr.____, taught him to be. And then we learn that Mr.____ is awful to women because that is what *his* father forced him to be. Harpo, left to himself, would have been happy cooking, watching the kids, doing the housework for his amazon wife. . . . Celie, in short, redeems these men by giving them the courage to be women, by releasing the woman already in them. But masculinity is unredeemable; masculinity is radical evil, irreducible, the causeless cause of all that's wrong in the world.

Such a view of men informs many recent novels and short stories, tales of a woman who leaves an impossible husband or lover or father, only to suffer further indignities at the hands of other lustful men, finally to find happiness or at least health in the embrace of a career (usually artistic), or another woman, or, in a few cases, in cohabitation with a homosexual male, a man happy to grant the heroine a room of her own, "preferably one with a key and a *lock*," as Alice Walker puts it.

These fictions, written over the last twenty years, since about the time Sylvia Plath's *The Bell Jar* was published, are an advance over their womanist predecessors in at least one way: no glamorous male is awarded to the heroine as a prize for her virtue; the rejection of men and all their ways is at last explicit—is, in fact, the conclusion and climax toward which everything else in these works tends. But these works also, in a number of ways, revert to their predecessors, to their narcissism, their sentimentality, their melodrama, their championing of domesticity over the public world of masculine power plays, and their nondenominational religiosity (*The Color Purple* is dedicated "To the Spirit: without whose assistance neither this book not I would have been written." Celie, Nettie, and Shug all pay their tribute to the Spirit. "God is everything, says Shug.")

No one can accuse Alice Walker of a failure of nerve—which may be why *The Color Purple* has meant so much more to American readers of fiction, the majority of whom are still women, than have the recent novels of Roth, Bellow, and Heller. For the sake of those contraries without which there is no progression, I would rather have manist writers bare their fangs than hide behind a sheepish grin. They can be sure that womanist writers will no longer pucker up, whatever the manists do.

—George Stade, "Womanist Fiction and Male Characters," *Partisan Review* 52, no. 3 (1985): pp. 264–270.

GERALD EARLY ON IDEOLOGICAL FAILURE

[Gerald Early is director and professor of African and Afro-American Studies at Washington University. He is the author of *Lure and Loathing* (1993), *Daughters: On Family and Fatherhood* (1994), and *How the War in the Streets Is Won* (poems, 1995). Early is crititical of *The Color Purple*, claiming that the novel "ultimately fails the ideology that it purports to serve."]

I have said that *The Color Purple* is not a good novel, but it does articulate one useful observation that I can dispense with quickly. The book utterly condemns the black male's glorification of his pimp mentality, and for this we should be thankful. For an insufferably long time, the black American male has been convinced, both by himself and by white males, that he is the monstrous stud on our cultural block. It is one of the few contemptible misrepresentations dreamed up by the white male that the black male has taken to heart, has clutched feverishly. Perhaps he has taken an unseemly pride in this perversion because it has titillated some white women (which in turn has titillated him) or because it has endowed him with the power of the slave master and permitted him to turn his community into a kind of brothel filled with "bitches" and "'ho'es." Whatever the case, Walker was quite right in linking that attempt to the oppressive attitude of the slave master, to the attitude of a rapist. It is appropriate that the lazy Mr. Albert should run something akin to a plantation with a big house as he remained a pimp in his soul.

Despite this, *The Color Purple* remains an inferior novel not because it seems so self-consciously a "woman's novel" and not because it may be playing down to its mass audience, guilty of being nothing more than a blatant "feel-good" novel, just the sort of book that is promoted among the nonliterary. *The Color Purple* is a poor novel because it ultimately fails the ideology that it purports to serve. It fails to be subversive enough in substance; it only *appears* to be subversive. Indeed, far from being a radically feminist novel, it is not even, in the end, as good a bourgeois feminist novel as *Uncle Tom's Cabin*, written 130 years earlier. Its largest failure lies in the novel's inability to use (ironically, subversively, or even interestingly) the elements that constitute it. Take, for instance, these various Victorianisms that abound in the work: the ultimate aim of the restoration of a gynocentric, not patriarchal family; the reunion of lost sisters; the reunion of mother and children; the glorification of cottage industry in the establishment of the pants business; bequests of money and land to the heroine at novel's end; Celie's discovery that her father/rapist is really a cruel stepfather; the change of heart or moral conversion of Mr. Albert, who becomes a feminized man by the end; the friendship between Shug Avery and Celie, which, despite its overlay of lesbianism (a tribute to James Baldwin's untenable thesis that nonstandard sex is the indication of a free, holy, thoroughly unsquare heterosexual heart), is nothing more than the typical relationship between a shy ugly duckling and her more aggressive, beautiful counterpart, a relationship not unlike that between Topsy and Little Eva. Shug convinces Celie that she is not black and ugly, that somebody loves her, which is precisely what Eva does for Topsy. For Walker, these clichés are not simply those of the Victorian novel but of the *woman's* Victorian novel. This indicates recognition of and paying homage to a tradition; but the use of these clichés in *The Color Purple* is a great deal more sterile and undemanding than their use in, say, *Uncle Tom's Cabin*. Together, for Walker, these clichés take on a greater attractiveness and power than for the female Victorian, since they are meant to represent a series of values that free the individual from the power of the environment, the whim of the state, and the orthodoxy of the institution. The individual still has the power to change, and that power supersedes all others, means more than any other. Human virtue is a reality that is not only distinct from all collective arrangements except family; in the end, it can be understood only as being opposed to all collective arrangements. But all of this is only the bourgeois fascination with individualism and with the ambiguity of Western family life, in which bliss is togetherness while having a room of one's own.

—Gerald Early, "*The Color Purple* as Everybody's Protest Art," *Antioch Review* (Summer 1986): pp. 270–275.

RICHARD WESLEY ON BLACK MEN

[Richard Wesley is a playwright whose works include the screenplay for *Uptown Saturday Night* (1990), *Let's Do It Again* (1991), and the plays *The Sirens* (1975) and *The Mighty Gents* (1979). Here, he discusses the division among African Americans over the message of *The Color Purple*.]

What angers black men as they read ⟨*The Color Purple*⟩, or watch the film version, is that *all* the black men are portrayed as fools; the women are portrayed as noble and long-suffering. If they have any weaknesses, they are weaknesses seemingly brought about by their long association with these foolish men. Walker had a point to make, and she had no need to include those black men who, with the help of the women in their lives, raised large families, sent their children off to school and into productive lives.

Black people from poor, impoverished southern rural backgrounds can tell endless stories about such men. They were not from middle-class backgrounds, nor did they have much in the way of education. They lived just down the road from where Celie and Mister lived. Many black women were upset that Alice Walker chose to paint a picture in which these men did not exist. I was not "upset," but I was disappointed.

We may understand the sociological conditions that might explain Mister, but there are some black men who are going to be brutes no matter what the circumstances of their lives. Mister behaves the way he does because he can get away with it. He has the power. He reflects the prevailing attitudes of male privilege. As long as black men seek to imitate the power structure that crushes them, as long as black women support this sad act of imitation and intimidation, and as long as black women submit to the idea that they have done something to deserve a lowly status in life and in the eyes of their husbands, then the morbid relationship of Celie, the oppressed, and Mister, the oppressed oppressor, will continue to be played out in homes all across America.

My feelings about *The Color Purple* put me directly at odds with many black artists, social leaders, civic leaders, and ordinary citizens all over the United States who *do* have enormous problems with the novel and with the film. That is their prerogative and I respect it.

What I do not respect, however, is the behavior of others in my community who have taken it upon themselves to be guardians of the black image.

These image tribunes are most often black males, usually in their thirties and older. They almost always seem to base their attacks on political concepts developed in the community during the turbulent days of the 1960s. For these men, the Black Power ideology of that time has remained sacrosanct and is in no need of revision. Part of that ideology requires black men and women to pull together. However, the unity of black men and women can only exist if the man *leads.* Therefore the woman must "submit": remain silent on sensitive issues. You do not "disrespect" your man in public, that is, criticize him in public, or speak too loudly about things that matter to you, or interrupt him when he is conversing with friends or colleagues on "serious" issues. A woman must always defer to her man and subjugate her will to his.

Few black men in their right minds will come out and couch their objections to Walker's novel in those terms, but you can hear echoes of those sentiments in much of their criticism of her: Walker is airing dirty linen in public. She is reminding many of us men of our own failures. She is reminding women of *their* failures as well. She is saying that Black is Beautiful, but not necessarily always *right.* A lot of people do not want to hear that.

> —Richard Wesley, "'*The Color Purple*' Debate: Reading Between the Lines," *Ms.* 15, no. 3 (September 1986): pp. 62, 90–92.

DARRYL PINCKNEY ON THE LIBERATING BONDS BETWEEN BLACK WOMEN

[Darryl Pinckney writes for the *New York Review of Books* and is author of a novel, *High Cotton* (1993). In this essay he discusses the characters of Celie and her sister, Nettie.]

The Color Purple is an epistolary novel. Celie, age fourteen, writes letters to "God." She has no one else to talk to about her troubles, of which she has plenty. ⟨. . .⟩ Celie is condemned to a life of drudgery because she is ugly, poor, black, and a woman. She is married off to a "Mr._____" ⟨. . .⟩ who has more brats than he let on. . . . Most of the novel concerns the downs of Celie's life with her new family and her long campaign to free herself.

The agent of Celie's salvation is a "high-natured" blues singer, a woman called Shug, who is Mister's lifelong obsession and who becomes Celie's great love as well. ⟨. . .⟩

Celie isn't shy before the Lord. The letters are rendered in a folk idiom, not as someone like Celie would probably compose them, and one wonders why Walker did not let Celie tell her story directly as an innocent narrator.

In addition to Celie's racy missives, the novel consists of letters from Nettie, Celie's beloved little sister who runs away from their pa only to be turned out by Celie's husband after fighting him off. The earnest Nettie writes to Celie from Africa where she has gone to be a missionary with a couple who just so happen also to be the adoptive parents of Celie's two children. However, Mister intercepts Nettie's letters. Celie, with Shug's help, finds Nettie's letters in a trunk and the realization that Mister has kept them from her for some twenty years leads her to vote with her feet for freedom.

The use of Africa in the novel points to the programmatic intention behind Walker's design. The motherland is celebrated: "Did you know there were great cities in Africa, greater than Milledgeville or even Atlanta, thousands of years ago?" Blackness per se is also honored. ⟨. . .⟩ In between descriptions of plantings and other rituals, Nettie is critical of patriarchy, of the limited choices for women in her village, and of the practice of clitorectomy. Walker manages not to miss any bases in the correct-line department, and perhaps that is why Nettie's letters seem stiff when compared to Celie's back-fence gossip with the Lord.

Nettie is also something of a historical anachronism. The American Missionary Association trained most of its black evangelicals in the late nineteenth century. The example of Nora A. Gordon of Spelman College, who was compelled by "Christ's preciousness" to "take the Bread of Life to the poor heathen," inspired black women students in the last century not only because being a missionary was a dramatic gesture of racial uplift but also because it was an acceptable expression of ambition, a way out. But funds for and belief in the missionary vocation declined sharply after the turn of the century, and women like Mary McLeod Bethune and Alice Dunbar-Nelson became educators or worked in the black woman's club movement instead. Nettie, not a Garveyite, would have been historically more convincing had she merely gone north.

Mainly, through the lives of Nettie and Celie, Walker means to say a great deal about the liberating possibilities of the bonds between black women. But she also means to say a lot about black men, those boulders obstructing the path to glory. ⟨. . .⟩

The black men are seen at a distance—that is, entirely from the point of view of the women—as naifs incapable of reflection, tyrants filled with impotent rage, or as totemic do-gooders. Walker's cards are always stacked against them—"Well, you know wherever there's a man, there's trouble"—even when her polemical intention is confused by her folksy tone. "A girl child ain't safe in a family of men." Contemporary black women's fiction has always contained scenes of domestic tension and even offhand domestic violence. But in *The Color Purple* this violence is on virtually every page. And throughout the novel, the color of the villains has changed, from white society to black men.

—Darryl Pinckney, "Black Victims, Black Villains," *New York Review of Books* 34, no. 1 (29 January 1987): pp. 17–20.

Deborah E. McDowell on the Linguistic Experience

[Deborah E. McDowell is professor of English and African-American Studies at the University of Virginia. She is author of *The Changing Same: Studies in Fiction by Black Women* (1994) and *Slavery and the Literary Imagination* (1988). Here she discusses Celie's letters to God in *The Color Purple*.]

Celie begins her story at age fourteen in the form of letters to God, the only one who can hear her, she thinks. Feeling isolated and ashamed, she tells Him of her life of brutality and exploitation at the hands of men. Writing is all-important to Celie; her last resounding word to her sister Nettie before they separate is "Write."

While Celie's letters are an attempt to communicate with someone outside herself, they also reveal a process of self-examination and self-discovery in much the same way the letter functioned for the protagonists in Richardson's *Clarissa* and *Pamela*. In other words, Celie's growth is chartable through her letters to God, which are essentially letters of self-exploration, enabling her to become connected to her thoughts and feelings. That connection eventually liberates her from a belief in a God outside herself, whom she has always imagined as "Big and old and tall and graybearded and white," and acquaints her with the God inside herself.

The spiritual dimension of Celie's discovery of the God-in-self has striking implications for her experience as a writer—for a writer she is, first and foremost. A self-reflexive novel, *The Color Purple* explicitly allegorizes much about the process and problematics of writing for the black woman. For example, the process by which Celie comes to shift her addressee from God to Nettie suggests much about the relationship between writer and audience and its effect on narrative authority and autonomy, to forceful voice. *The Color Purple* makes clear that the black woman writer has written primarily without an audience capable of accepting and appreciating that the full, raw, unmediated range of the black woman's story could be appropriate subject matter for art.

The Celie letters addressed to God indicate that she is a writer without an audience, without a hearing, a predicament she recognizes only after discovering that her husband has intercepted and hidden in a trunk letters her sister Nettie has written to her from Africa over a thirty-year period. As Celie recovers from the shock, she announces to Shug that she has ceased to write to God, now realizing that "the God I had been praying and writing to is a man. And act just like all the other mens I know. Trifling, forgitful, and low-down." When Shug cautions Celie to be quiet, lest God hear her, Celie responds defiantly, "Let 'im hear me, I say. If he ever listened to poor colored women the world would be a different place."

Celie's decision to cease writing to God and to begin writing to her sister Nettie marks a critical point in both her psychological development and in her development as a writer. Significantly, before Celie discovers that God is not listening, her letters to him record passive resignation, silence, and blind faith in his benevolence. She can suffer abuses in this life, she confides to Sophia, because "⟨it⟩ soon be over. . . . Heaven last all ways." In these letters, she identifies with Squeak who speaks in a "little teenouncy voice." She "stutters," "mutters"; her "throat closes," and "nothing come⟨s⟩ out but a little burp." Celie admits that she "can't fix ⟨her⟩ mouth to say how ⟨she⟩ feel⟨s⟩." Appropriately, these letters record a distinct split between what she thinks and what she feels and says. For example, when Nettie leaves for Africa, she expresses sadness at leaving Celie to be buried by the burden of caring for Mr.____ and his children. Celie writes, "It's worse than that, I think. If I was buried, I wouldn't have to work. But I just say, Never mine, never mine, long as I can spell G-o-d I got somebody along." Similarly, when Celie thinks she sees her daughter Olivia at the drygoods store in town, she strikes up a conversation with the woman who has custody of the child. The woman makes a joke about the child's name, and Celie writes: "I git it and laugh. It feel like to split my face." The image of the split functions here, as in so many novels by women, as a sign of the character's tenuous sense of self, of identity, if you will. The image objectifies the split between Celie's outer and inner selves that will ultimately be made whole as the novel develops.

It is further significant that none of the letters addressed to God is signed. In their anonymity, their namelessness, the letters further underscore Celie's lack of individuality. When she begins to write to Nettie, however, her inner and outer selves become connected. Her thoughts are fused with her feelings, her actions, her words, and the letters assume a quality of force and authority, at times of prophecy, as seen in Celie's conversation with Mr.____ before she leaves for Memphis:

> Until you do right by me, everything you touch will crumble.
> He laugh. Who you think you is? he say. You can't curse nobody. Look at you. You black, you pore, you ugly, you a woman. Goddamn, he say, you nothing at all.
> Until you do right by me, I say, everything you even dream about will fail.

Celie concludes: "I'm pore, I'm black, I may be ugly and can't cook. . . . But I'm here." Thus these letters addressed to Nettie are alternately signed "Your sister, Celie" and "Amen," expressions of ratification, of approval, of assertion, of validation. The suggestion is clear: Celie is now ratifying, asserting, and validating her own words, her own worth, and the authority of her own experience. Celie's validation of her linguistic experience is especially important, for it is so critical to the establishment of her own literary voice.

—Deborah E. McDowell, "(The Changing Same): Generational Connections and Black Novelists," *New Literary History* 18, no. 2 (Winter 1987). Reprinted in *Alice Walker*, ed. Harold Bloom (New York: Chelsea House, 1989): pp. 143–145.

[Bell Hooks (Gloria Watkins) teaches English and African-American literature at Yale University. She is author of *Bone Black: Memories of Girlhood* (1996), *Art on My Mind* (1995), *Black Looks: Race and Representation* (1992), and *Breaking Bread: Insurgent Black Intellectual Life* (1991). In this work, Hooks discusses the characters in *The Color Purple*.]

Characters are very much what they do in *The Color Purple*. Mr.____ is brute, Lucious the rapist, Harpo the buffoon, Celie the sexual victim, Shug the sexual temptress. Many of the characters perform roles that correspond with racial stereotypes. The image of "the black male rapist" resonates in both racial and sexual stereotypes; Walker's characterization cannot be viewed in a vacuum, as though it does not participate in these discourses which have been primarily used to reinforce domination, both racial and sexual.

Pornography participates in and promotes a discourse that exploits and aesthetizes domination. Kuhn asserts that pornography insists on sexual difference, that sexual violence in master-slave scenarios reduces this difference to relations of power. Feminists who focus almost exclusively on male violence against women as the central signifier of male domination also view sexual difference as solely a relation of power. Within pornography, Kuhn states, there is

> an obsession with the otherness of femininity, which in common with many forms of otherness seems to contain a threat to the onlooker. Curiosity turns to terror, investigation to torture, the final affirmation of the objecthood of the other. The feminine here represents a threat to the masculine, a threat which demands containment. Sexually violent pornography of this kind concretises this wish for containment in representations which address the spectator as masculine and place the masculine on the side of container of the threat. It insists that sexuality and power are inseparable.

Walker inverts this paradigm. Presuming a female spectator (women and specifically white women from privileged classes are the primary audience for women-centered novels), she constructs a fiction in which it is the masculine threat, represented by black masculinity, that must be contained, controlled, and ultimately transformed. Her most radical re-visioning of the oppressive patriarchal social order is her insistence on the transformation of Mr.____. He moves from male oppressor to enlightened being, willingly surrendering his attachment on the phallocentric social order reinforced by the sexual oppression of women. His transformation begins when Celie threatens his existence, when her curse disempowers him. Since sexuality and power are so closely linked to politics of domination, Mr.____ must be completely desexualized as part of the transformative process.

Unable to reconcile sexuality and power, Walker replaces the longing for sexual pleasure with an erotic metaphysic animated by a vision of the unity of all things, by the convergence of erotic and mystical experience. This is ritually enacted as Shug initiates Celie into a spiritual awakening wherein belief in God as white male authority figure, who gives orders and punishes, is supplanted by the vision of a loving God who wants believer to celebrate life, to experience pleasure, a God who is annoyed, "if you walk by the color purple in a field somewhere but don't notice it." In *The Color Purple* Christianity and patriarchy are oppressive social structures which promote anhedonia. Celie and Albert, as oppressed and oppressor, must as part of their personal transformation learn to feel pleasure and develop a capacity to experience happiness. Concurrently, Nettie and Samuel, laboring as missionaries in Africa, develop a critical consciousness that allows them to see the connections between Western cultural imperialism and Christianity; and this enables them to see God in a new way. Nettie writes to Celie, "God is different to us now, after all these years in Africa, more spirit than even before, and more internal." Though critical of religious beliefs which reinforce sexist and racist domination, Shug insists on the primacy of a spiritual life, constructing a vision of spirituality which echoes the teachings of religious mystics who speak of healing alienation through recognition of the unity in all life.

Spiritual quest is connected with the effort of characters in *The Color Purple* to be more fully self-realized. This effort merges in an unproblematic way with a materialist ethic which links acquisition of goods with the capacity to experience emotional well-being. Traditionally mystical experience is informed by radical critique and renunciation of materialism. Walker positively links the two. Even though her pronounced critique of patriarchy includes an implicit indictment of perverse individualism which encourages exploitation (Albert is transformed in part by his rejection of isolation and self-sufficiency for connection and interdependency), Celie's shift from underclass victim to capitalist entrepreneur has only positive signification. Albert, in his role as oppressor, forces Celie and Harpo to work in the fields, exploiting their labor for his gain. Their exploitation a workers must cease before domination ends and transformation begins. Yet Celie's progression from exploited black woman, as woman, as sexual victim, is aided by her entrance into the economy as property owner, manager of a small business, storekeeper—in short, capitalist entrepreneur. No attention is accorded aspects of this enterprise that might reinforce domination: attention is focused on how useful Celie's pants are for family and friends; on the way Sophia as worker in her store will treat black customers with respect and consideration. Embedded in the construction of sexual difference as it is characterized in *The Color Purple* is the implicit assumption that women are innately less inclined to oppress and dominate than men; that women are not easily corrupted.

—Bell Hooks, "Writing the Subject: Reading *The Color Purple*," in *Alice Walker*, ed. Harold Bloom (New York: Chelsea House, 1988): 215–228.

Works by
Alice Walker

Once (poems), 1968.

The Third Life of Grange Copeland, 1970.

Revolutionary Petunias and Other Poems, 1973.

In Love and Trouble: Stories of Black Women, 1973.

Langston Hughes: American Poet, 1974.

Meridian, 1976.

Good Night, Willie Lee, I'll See You in the Morning (poems), 1979.

You Can't Keep a Good Woman Down, 1981.

The Color Purple, 1982.

In Search of Our Mothers' Gardens: Womanist Prose, 1983.

Horses Make a Landscape More Beautiful (poems), 1984.

Living by the Word, 1988.

The Temple of My Familiar, 1989.

Her Blue Body Everything We Know (poems), 1991.

Possessing the Secret of Joy, 1992.

Works about
Alice Walker

Bloom, Harold, ed. *Alice Walker*. New York: Chelsea House, 1989.

Bobo, Jacqueline. "Sifting Through Controversy: Reading *The Color Purple*." *Callaloo* 12, no. 2 (Spring 1989): 332–342.

——. "*The Color Purple*: Black Women as Cultural Readers." In *Female Spectators: Looking at Film and Television*, ed. Deidre Pribram. London: Verso, 1988.

Butler, C. B. "*The Color Purple* Controversy—Black Woman Spectatorship." *Wide Angle: A Quarterly Journal of Film History Theory and Criticism* 13, no. 3–4 (1991): 62–69.

Christian, Barbara. "No More Buried Lives: The Theme of Lesbianism in Lorde, Naylor, Shange, Walker." *Feminist Issues* 5, no. 1 (Spring 1985): 3–20.

——. "The Contrary Black Women of Alice Walker." *Black Scholar* 12, no. 2 (March–April 1981): 21–30, 70–71.

Coles, Robert. "To Try Men's Souls." *The New Yorker* (27 February 1971): 104–106.

Cooke, Michael G. "Alice Walker: The Centering Self." In *Afro-American Literature in the Twentieth Century*. New Haven: Yale University Press, 1984, pp. 157–176.

Digby, Joan. "From Walker to Spielberg: Transformations of *The Color Purple*." In *Novel Images: Literature in Performance*, ed. Peter Reynolds. London: Routledge, 1993, pp. 157–174.

Dole, Carol M. "The Return of the Father in Spielberg's *The Color Purple*." *Literature Film Quarterly* 24, no. 1 (January 1996): 12–16.

DuPlessis, Rachel Blau. *Writing Beyond the Ending: Narrative Strategies of Twentieth Century Women Writers*. Bloomington: Indiana University Press, 1985.

Fifer, Elizabeth. "The Dialect and Letters of *The Color Purple*." In *Contemporary American Women Writers: Narrative Strategies*, ed. Catherine Rainwater and William J. Scheick. Lexington: University Press of Kentucky, 1985, pp. 155–165.

Fowler, Carolyn. "Solid at the Core." *Freedomways* 14 (1974): 59–62.

Froula, Christine. "The Daughter's Seduction: Sexual Violence and Literary History." *Signs* 11 (1986): 621–645.

Harris, Trudier. "Folklore in the Fiction of Alice Walker: A Perpetuation of Historical and Literary Traditions." *Black American Literature Forum* 11 (1977): 3–8.

Heirs, John T. "Creation Theology in Alice Walker's *The Color Purple.*" *Notes on Contemporary Literature* 14, no. 4 (September 1984): 2–3.

Iannone, Carol. "A Turning of the Critical Tide?" *Commentary* 88, no. 5 (November 1989): 57–59.

Lenhart, Georgann. "Inspired Purple?" *Notes on Contemporary Literature* 14, no. 3 (May 1984): 2–3.

McGowen, Martha J. "Atonement and Release in Alice Walker's *Meridian.*" *Critique* 23 (1981): 25–35.

Meese, Elizabeth A. "Defiance: The Body (of) Writing/The Writing (of) the Body." In *Crossing the Double-Cross: The Practice of Feminist Criticism.* Chapel Hill: University of North Carolina Press, 1986.

Peacock, J. "When Folk Goes Pop—Consuming *The Color Purple:* Afro-American Folklore, Contemporary American Culture and the Spielberg Film." *Literature Film Quarterly* 19, no. 3 (1991): 176–180.

Pryse, Marjorie. "Zora Neale Hurston, Alice Walker, and the Ancient Power of Black Women." In *Conjuring: Black Women, Fiction, and the Literary Tradition*, ed. Marjorie Pryse and Hortense Spillers. Bloomington: Indiana University Press, 1985, pp. 1–24.

Shelon, F. W. "Alienation and Integration in Alice Walker's *The Color Purple.*" *CLA Journal* 28 (1985): 382–392.

Stein, Kara F. "*Meridian:* Alice Walker's Critique of Revolution." *Black American Literature Forum* 20 (1986): 129–241.

Tate, Claudia. "Alice Walker." In *Black Women Writers at Work*, ed. Claudia Tate. New York: Continuum, 1983, pp. 175–187.

Washington, Mary Helen. "An Essay on Alice Walker." In *Sturdy Black Bridges: Visions of Black Women in Literature,* ed. Roseann P. Bell, Bettye J. Parker, and Beverly Guy-Sheftall. Garden City, N.Y.: Doubleday (Anchor), 1979, pp. 133–149.

———. "I Sign My Mother's Name: Alice Walker, Dorothy West, Paule Marshall." In *Mothering the Mind: Twelve Studies of Writers and Their Silent Partners,* ed. Ruth Perry and Martine Watson Brownley. New York: Holmes & Meier, 1984, pp. 142–163.

Watkins, Mel. "Sexism, Racism, and Black Women Writers." *The New York Times Book Review* (15 June 1986): 1, 35–37.

———. "Some Letters Went to God." *The New York Times Book Review* (25 July 1982): 7.

Williams, D. S. "*The Color Purple.*" *Christianity and Crisis* (14 July 1986): 230–232.

Index of
Themes and Ideas